Work in Process
an image & tutorial collection
kamui 2008

All rights reserved.
Copyright © 2008 by kamui.

ISBN 978-90-79082-09-4

Published by Bad Dog Books
www.baddogbooks.com

Printed by FurPlanet in the U.S.A.
www.furplanet.com

Preface

Every artist has their own reason for pursuing their craft; that spark that pushes them to take a pencil to a stack of dead trees or go half-blind chasing electrons around a screen.

Motives range from the love of money to divine inspiration, but most of us tend to find ourselves somewhere in the middle. My driving interest lies in illustration as storytelling—creating a visual narrative that conveys a time, a place, a personality, an emotion—and at the heart of all storytelling is communication. Without an audience, the story ends with me.

Even when fortunate enough to find an audience, however, the conversation often ends after the artist has spoken his peace and the viewer heard him out. In most cases, the artist is never a party to the viewer's reactions. Even in the lucky cases where feedback is possible, it can be difficult to describe the experience of viewing art in written language. Inevitably, the exchange remains limited, fleeting.

Well then, how to prolong and expand upon that communication? In putting together this collection of images, I wanted to push beyond the unilateral exchange. I hoped to put together a book that could serve to spark dialogue. Specifically, I wanted people to see my work, and be driven to make their own art.

As I saw it, that left me with two options. One, to put together a collection of works so unstoppably amazing that onlookers would be inspired to drop everything and create on the spot, whether they like it or not. In addition to being totally beyond my abilities, I tend to favor a somewhat softer touch.

The second was to make a book about making art; a collection of the ideas, conventions, and specific techniques that I use when creating. My hope is that by explaining how it is I do what I do, people will see how easy (which is often "embarrassingly") it is, and be motivated to go try some of it out by making art that's fun and meaningful for them.

So, firm in my resolve, I sat down to put together this book, which holds a dozen or so illustrations and a step-by-step look at some of the processes that went into creating them.

All of the images collected here were made in 2007-2008, using Adobe® Photoshop® CS2 software and a Wacom® Intuos2 tablet. While many artists have access to these wonderful tools, I realize that not everyone has a full digital studio at their fingertips. Though I'll be speaking specifically about how I make my art in Photoshop, I hope a good portion of what I have to say here can be readily applied to any medium, be it pencils, oils, or clay.

The vast majority of the creative process happens somewhere between the brain and the hand, and, at the end of the day, learning the universals of art (things like line, perspective, color, and anatomy come readily to mind) and training the arm are both infinitely more important than knowing what filter to use when and similar technical minutiae.

...But those take forever, so I'll be including some quick tips here and there for cheap thrills anyway.

First and foremost, I hope you enjoy this book. As its author, I'm excited at the prospect of seeing art from readers that uses some of these techniques, or better yet adapts and evolves them into something utterly new and unique that I can then learn from in turn.

I'll be eagerly awaiting those reactions; calls echoing back in response from the void that usually awaits an artist's work. Tell me your stories!

—THE ARTIST

> **Whereas it doesn't get much simpler than pulling a line with charcoal on paper, digital art is a roiling cauldron of black box technology mixed with even blacker magic. While I couldn't begin to tell you HOW this stuff works, I can at least tell you a bit about WHY.**

at the market
the concept

It all starts with an idea.
Ideally a *good* one, but we make do with what we've got.

Work put into thinking through an image before putting pencil to paper can do a lot more towards making the finished piece a success than any amount of obsessive detailing at the end, and can wind up saving you time and effort along the way by spotting potential problems and avoiding them before they happen.

More than a specific theme or characters, this picture was about an idea. Under normal circumstances, The Rules clearly say that a shot should be framed to best showcase the action taking place within it. Well, what happens if you purposefully break that and obscure the focal point of the scene?

My general policy with breaking The Rules is "take a little, give a little." I was curious to push the envelope a bit, but wanted to make sure all the information was still there if you were looking for it. That lead me to the idea of using indirect reflection, which then lead me to puddles, which gradually lead to the whole post-shower farmers' market scene.

I guess sometimes you start at the punch line and figure out the joke in reverse.

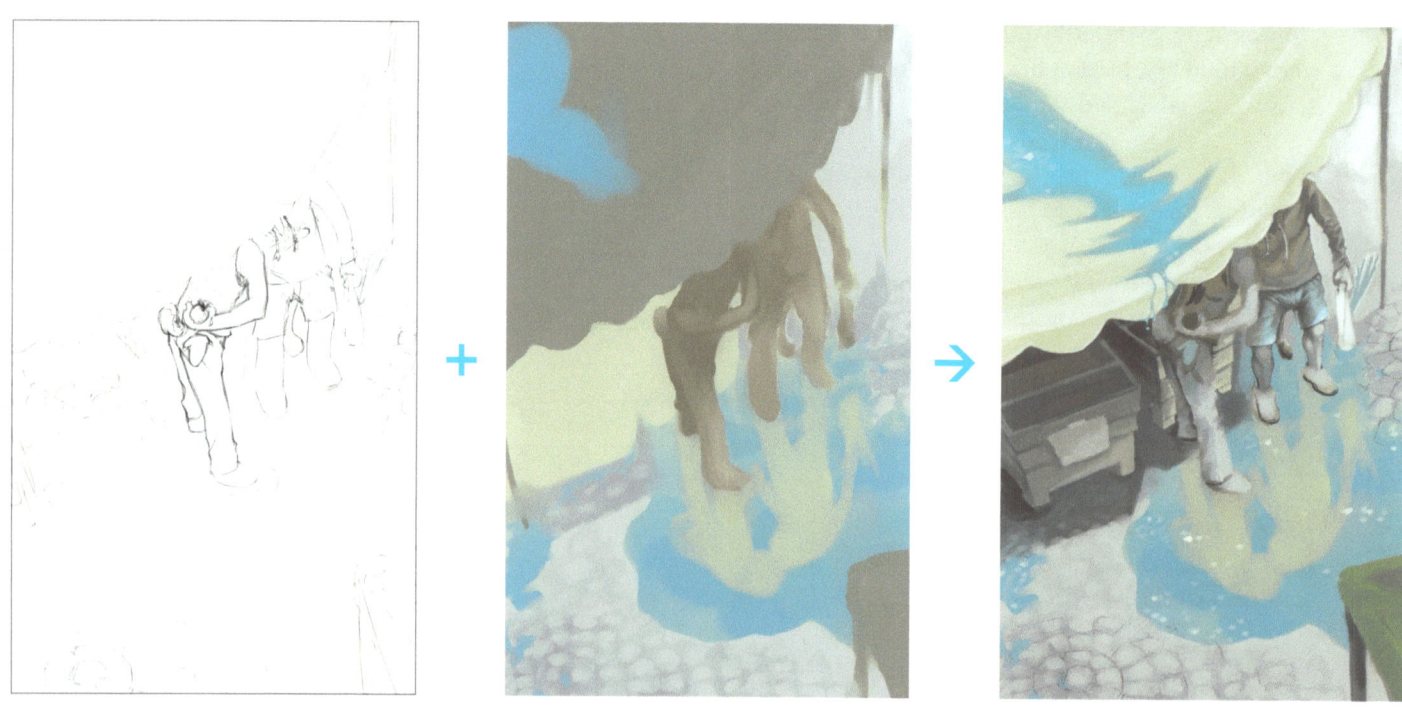

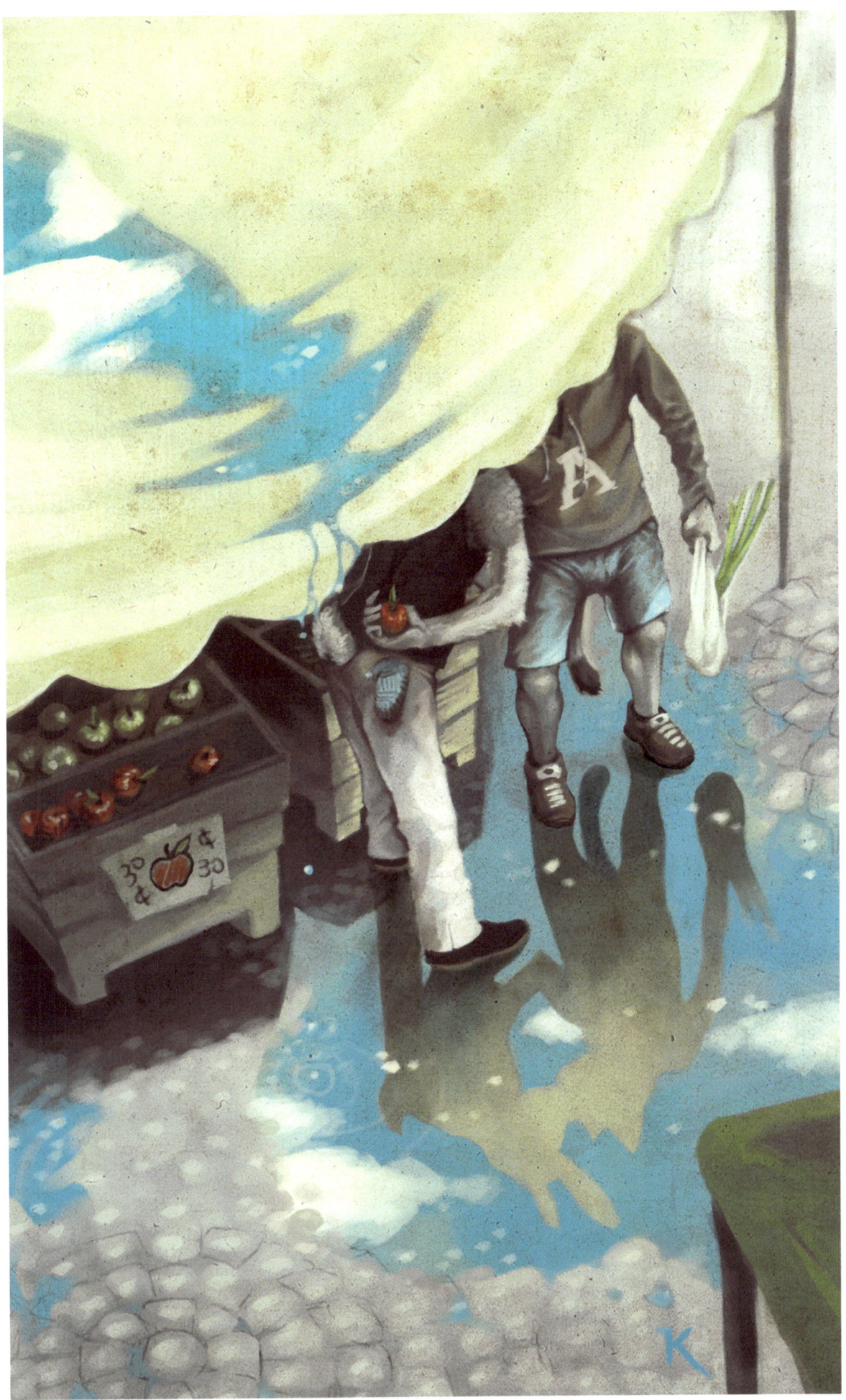

Well, I'm afraid that Photoshop can't really help you come up with a killer concept for your next brilliant piece, so let's spend a minute getting used to workspace, shall we?

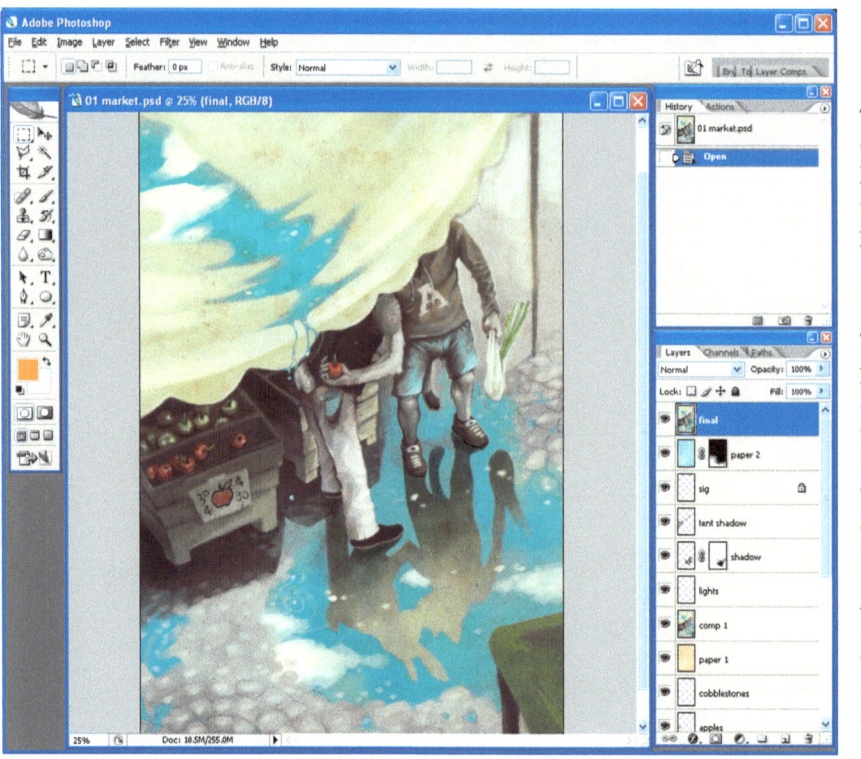

See a detailed description of the tools I use below, or poke around and see for yourself what does what!

Fresh apples for just ¢30! A tasty deal by any account.

The history palette keeps track of your actions and lets you to jump back in time whenever you feel you've gone off track.

The layers palette allows you to build a stack of rearrangeable, independently editable layers that allow you make changes to parts of your piece while leaving the rest of it intact.

A host of layer blending modes provide an easy way to achieve a broad spectrum of lighting and color effects.

(M) marquee (select) move (V)
(L) lasso

brush (B)
(S) rubber stamp history brush (Y)
(E) eraser gradient (G)
(R) sharpen & blur dodge & burn (O)

(P) pen shape (U)
eyedropper (I)
(H) hand zoom (Z)

(X: toggle) active colors

I know most folks already know their way around this beast, but for the folks who are just starting out, I'll spend a couple of pages describing the parts that I use to do what I do.

The marquee and lasso tools are used to make specific selections within your image, allowing you to cordon off that portion while painting, relocate the selected piece within the image, or apply transformations such as re-scaling or rotating, perfect for correcting little mistakes in pose and proportion.

Holding the SHIFT key while using a selection tool will add to your existing selection, while holding the ALT key will subtract from it. Using these shortcuts on the fly can make getting your selection just right a whole lot faster.

Holding SHIFT with the marquee tool after you've clicked, while dragging a new selection, will lock the marquee into a regular shape (i.e., a perfect square for the rectangular marquee, or a circle for the ellipse).

With the freehand lasso you can draw your selection manually. Hold ALT while you let go of the mouse button to toggle to the polygon lasso and add straight edges to your selection. Holding SHIFT while using the polygon lasso will constrain your lines to 45° degree angles, perfect for selecting along horizontal or vertical lines.

The move tool does just that—it allows you to relocate the contents of a layer or selection to another spot in the image.

The brush tool is where all the magic happens. Right clicking anywhere on the active window will bring up the brush select dialogue, where you can choose your weapon, then just point and click, drag, and paint!

Holding SHIFT constrains the brush to 45° angles, and ALT will toggle to the eyedropper tool, which you can use to pick up the color from elsewhere on the screen to use as your active color.

The rubber stamp and history brush tools are a bit tricky, but they can let you do some amazing things. In short, they let you paint pixels from some other source (the target you set with the ALT key in the case of the rubber stamp, or a history state you've selected for the history brush). It's easier with these to play around and see for yourself. It'll blow your mind.

The eraser tool will remove pixel data from the active layer—if you're working on the *Background* layer, it will paint with the active background color. If you're on a higher layer, you'll erase a hole in that layer that will allow lower layers to show through.

The gradient tool will paint a perfect blend between two or more colors (your foreground and background active colors by default) along a linear or radial path, depending on which sub-tool you select. Great for lighting effects, and a cousin to the Gradient Map feature, which I'll touch on later.

Sharpen & blur allow you to paint areas into or out of focus. Just remember that you can blur clear images unrecognizable, but you can't sharpen unrecognizable images clear! It's a one-way street, folks.

Dodge & burn simulate the photo processes where areas of an image are selectively underexposed (dodged) or overexposed (burned). In simple terms, dodge makes things brighter, while burn makes them darker. They're useful for deepening existing shadows or brightening highlights, but using them too much will make your image flat, oversaturated, and gross.

Hold ALT while using one to toggle it for the other.

The pen and shape tools are a bit tricky at first, too, but I'll be chatting more about them later on. For now, know that they draw paths based on mathematical formulae which can be used for a host of different purposes.

The hand and zoom tools are used to navigate your document, and don't alter the image at all. The hand lets you grab and scroll to different areas of the image, while the magnifying glass lets you zoom in and out.

The best keyboard shortcut in Photoshop is right here. Hold the SPACE BAR in any other tool to toggle to the hand, or SPACE BAR and SHIFT for zoom in or ALT for zoom out. Being able to navigate your image without changing tools saves a *ton* of time.

Lastly, your active colors are displayed with foreground color (which is what the brush tool lays down) on top. Click on the boxes to choose different colors from the RGB square, or use the eyedropper.

Hit X to switch foreground and background colors, or D to reset your active colors to black and white.

The history palette can save your ass. If you decide you want to go back to a previous state, just click on that state, and every horrifying mistake you made after that disappears as if it never happened at all.

You can also press CTRL+Z to Undo, but the history gives you a bit more of a hands-on feel, letting you compare and contrast even distant history states.

Just be careful—once a state disappears off the top of the list, it's gone for good, and you won't be able to jump back to it. If you're going to take a detour and try something crazy, either save a separate copy of the file, or take a snapshot by clicking on the camera icon at the bottom of the palette. Snapshots are like history states that never go away. Pretty awesome.

Check the box to the left of a history state to use it as the target for the history brush.

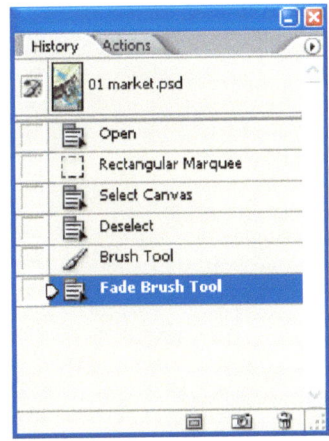

To make a new layer, click on the sticky note at the bottom of the palette. From there, you're ready to paint away without worry of messing up the information saved on another layer.

To rename a layer, double-click on its existing name. Calling it something more specific than "Layer 17" is invaluable to staying organized.

Dialogue boxes at the top let you set the layer's blending mode (more on those later) and opacity. Drag and drop a layer within the palette to rearrange its vertical position in the file. Opaque higher layers will cover up the information on lower layers, so stack them smartly!

Check or uncheck the eye icon to the left to toggle layer visibility, or, if you're permanently done with a layer, clean house by dragging it down to the trash can icon to delete it once and for all.

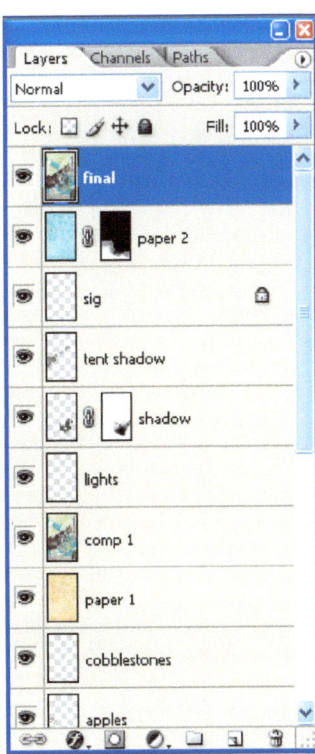

*rawk

sketching

Fear of messing up a perfectly nice sheet of blank paper
is reason no. 374 why I'm a digital artist.
Yes, I'm aware that it's ridiculous.

So everybody sketches differently. Even though I can count the number of sketchbooks I've filled in my career on approximately zero fingers, I still need a way to throw down visual ideas, either to remember for later, or to get the ball rolling on an image I'm starting now.

For the longest time, I understood "sketching" to mean "line drawing," but that's really just one of a broad range of sketching techniques out there to choose from. Personally, I've gravitated away from line recently because, frankly, I'm not very good at it. Linework is slow and arduous for me, but I can throw down patches of color in a few quick strokes that give me enough basic structure to work with as I build the rest of an image from there.

Again, an ounce of prevention is worth a pound of cure. Fix the problems in your sketch while it's still just a sketch! The more time and effort you funnel into a piece, the more reluctant you'll be to make sweeping changes to it, even if the image would be better off for them in the long run. Keeping things loose until you like where things are lying is sure to save you major headaches down the road.

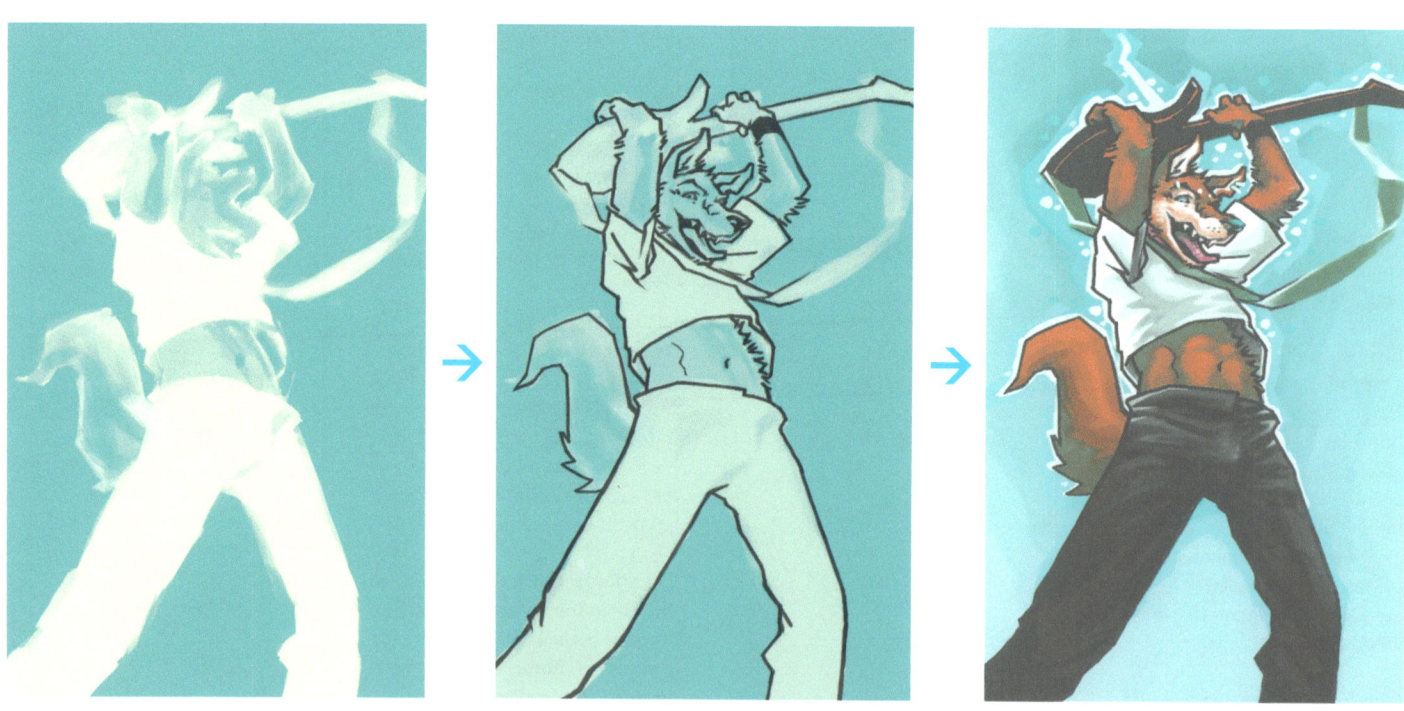

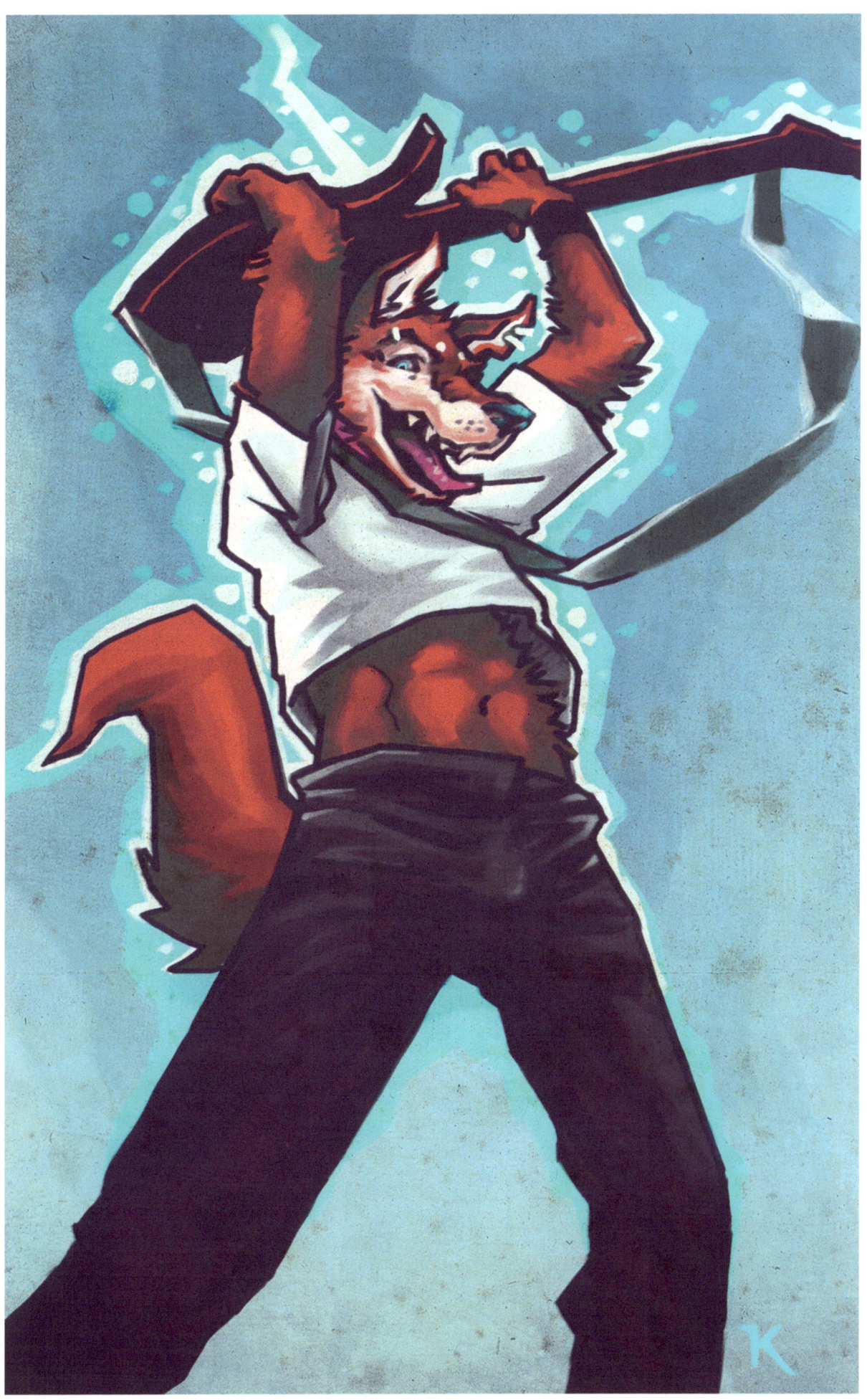

Okay, enough with the talking. Sketching is all about just getting in there and doing it, so here's a blow-by-blow of how I got the basics down on this image.

Ahh, the blank canvas...

So ripe with promise, so full of possibility... It's just crying out to have some amorphous, cheese-colored blob thrown on it.

I've got a big brush selected, and I'm just going to paint right onto my background layer. The sketch won't be a part of the final pic this time, so I'm not worried about putting it on a separate layer like I might do otherwise.

Let's rock!

Yes, this is really what all of my sketches look like at first.

...Shut up.

At this point I'm just blocking in the very roughest silhouette, getting a feel for how the pose and camera angle work.

If a different shot would work better, this is the perfect stage to make those changes!

Details lost in a sweeping change down the line means time and effort lost. The earlier you catch a problem, the less painful it'll be to fix it!

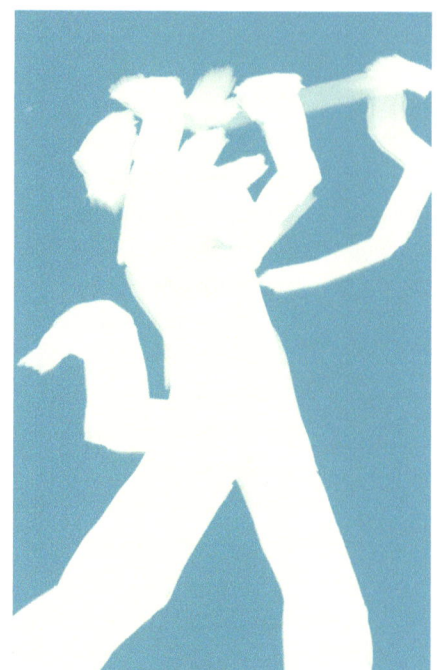

So my foreground color is set to cheese, and my background color is still at that steely blue background tone.

Now that I've got the rough silhouette down, I just start toggling back and forth between my foreground and background colors by hitting X on the keyboard—I find this quicker than jumping between the brush and eraser for the initial rough sketch.

I use the yellow to add and the blue to subtract, tightening up the silhouette some and starting to add in some very coarse detail.

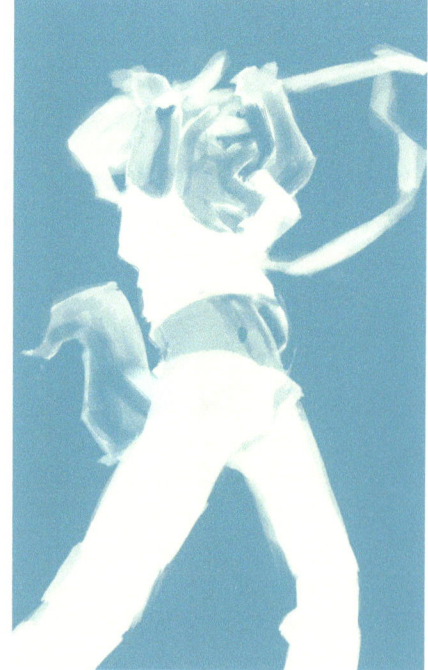

Now comes that new layer, blending mode set to Multiply, which adds the darkness and color of that layer to what's below it, making for an even darker combined total. It's handy when doing linework because it keeps your lines easy to see.

I grab a dark greyish color and start painting in some loose, chunky outlines.

This time, because I'm working on a new layer that I want to preserve as just outlines, I will want to toggle between the brush and eraser tools, getting rid of unwanted pixels completely rather than just making them the same color as the background.

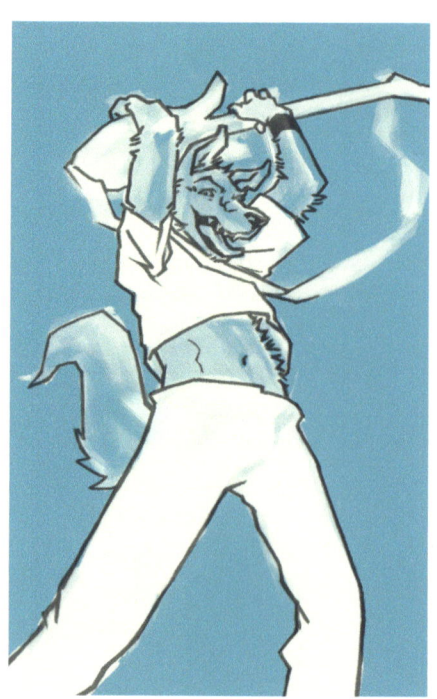

Making a new layer between my background rough and my lines and filling it with the same steely blue gives me a clean background for the finished picture without having to actually erase my sketch.

I usually like to keep the original sketch layer intact, just so I can see how I came at a picture later on.

I've also set my line layer to Normal so it stays a consistent tone no matter what's underneath it.

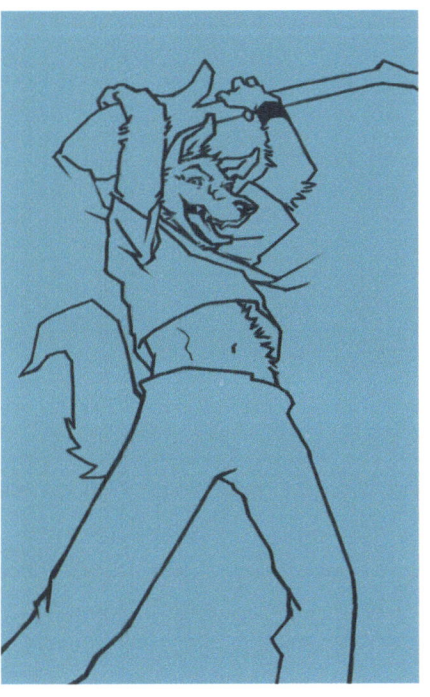

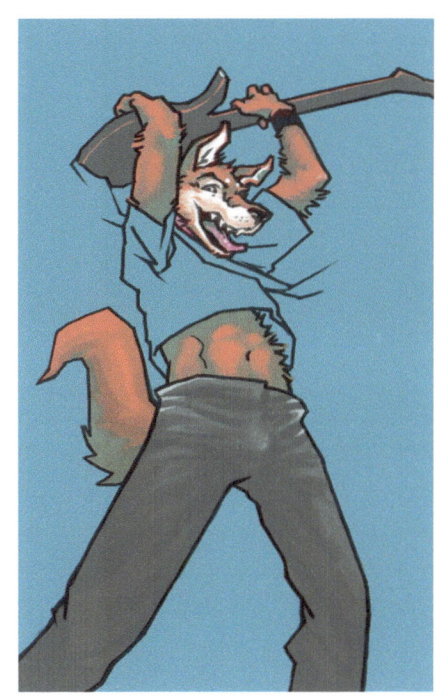

Next, I make more new layers underneath my lines; one for each major section. For this image, I had the fur on one layer, the pants and guitar on another, the guitar strap on a third, and our rocker's shirt on a fourth.

It needed more rock.

Typically, that means A) fire, B) lightning, or C) umlauts. This time I went with a bolt from the blue.

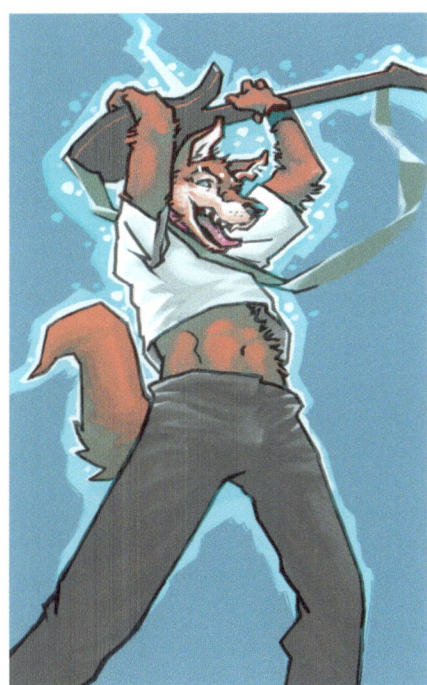

With the sketching portion pretty much done, all that was left was to put it through my usual gauntlet of texture layers and color adjustments.

I'll talk about all that a little later on, but this time around, the important part was definitely just getting nice and loose and chunky with a fast, free sketch.

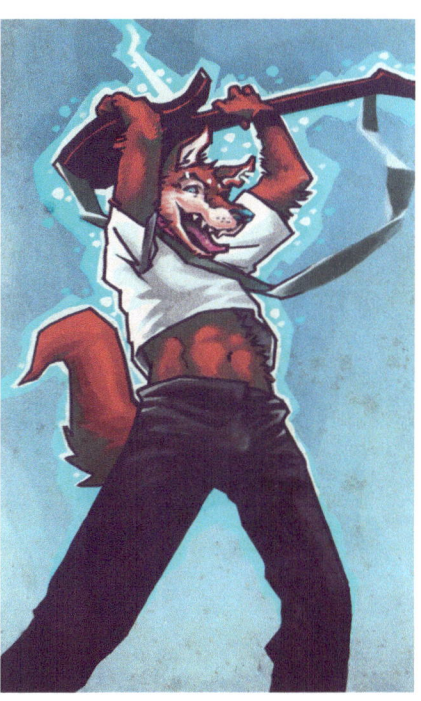

Even if your sketch lacks wailing guitars, try to remember to rock out in the process.

sunset
the brush

Many times, the image you want to make will dictate the tool you use.
Sometimes, the tool you just feel like using dictates the image.

The digital artist has a huge, essentially infinite set of painting tools at his disposal. If the preset brushes packaged with your software aren't cutting it, you can make your own. Experimenting with new and different brushes can open pathways to entirely new kinds of image-making techniques. Some work like pens, others like wet, diffuse watercolors, and still others like rubber stamps or photographic inlays—with the various settings available in the latest versions of several graphics applications, nearly any effect can be achieved.

I made this image immediately after working on a neurotic, obsessively detailed piece that had me pulling out my hair. I wanted to force myself NOT to get too finicky this time, so I created a custom brush with a purposefully unwieldy wedge shape, and tweaked the settings so that it would never dip below a generously sized minimum diameter. It was the digital equivalent of finger paints: fine control was simply not an option.

And I loved it. So much so that I've used that brush almost exclusively ever since. I've learned ways to use it with a lot more finesse than I managed in this first attempt, but I had fun, and remain happy with the roughness and energy my big brush left on its maiden voyage.

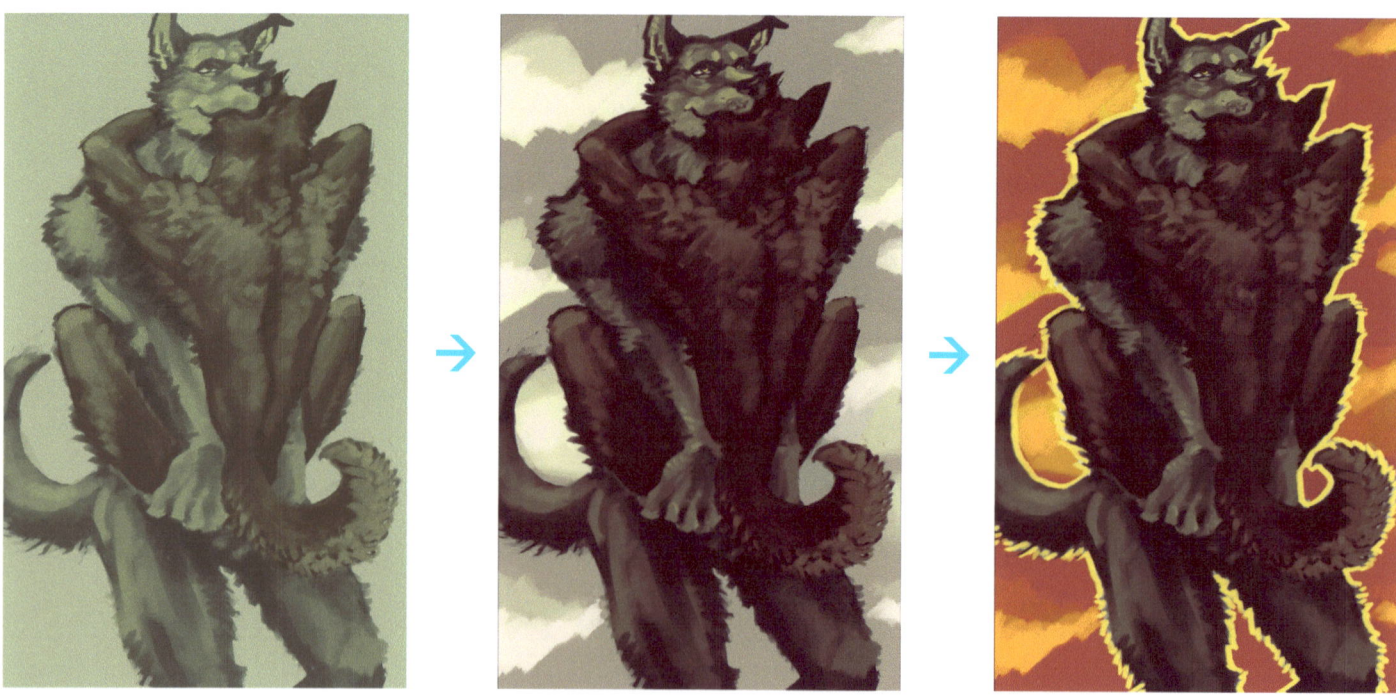

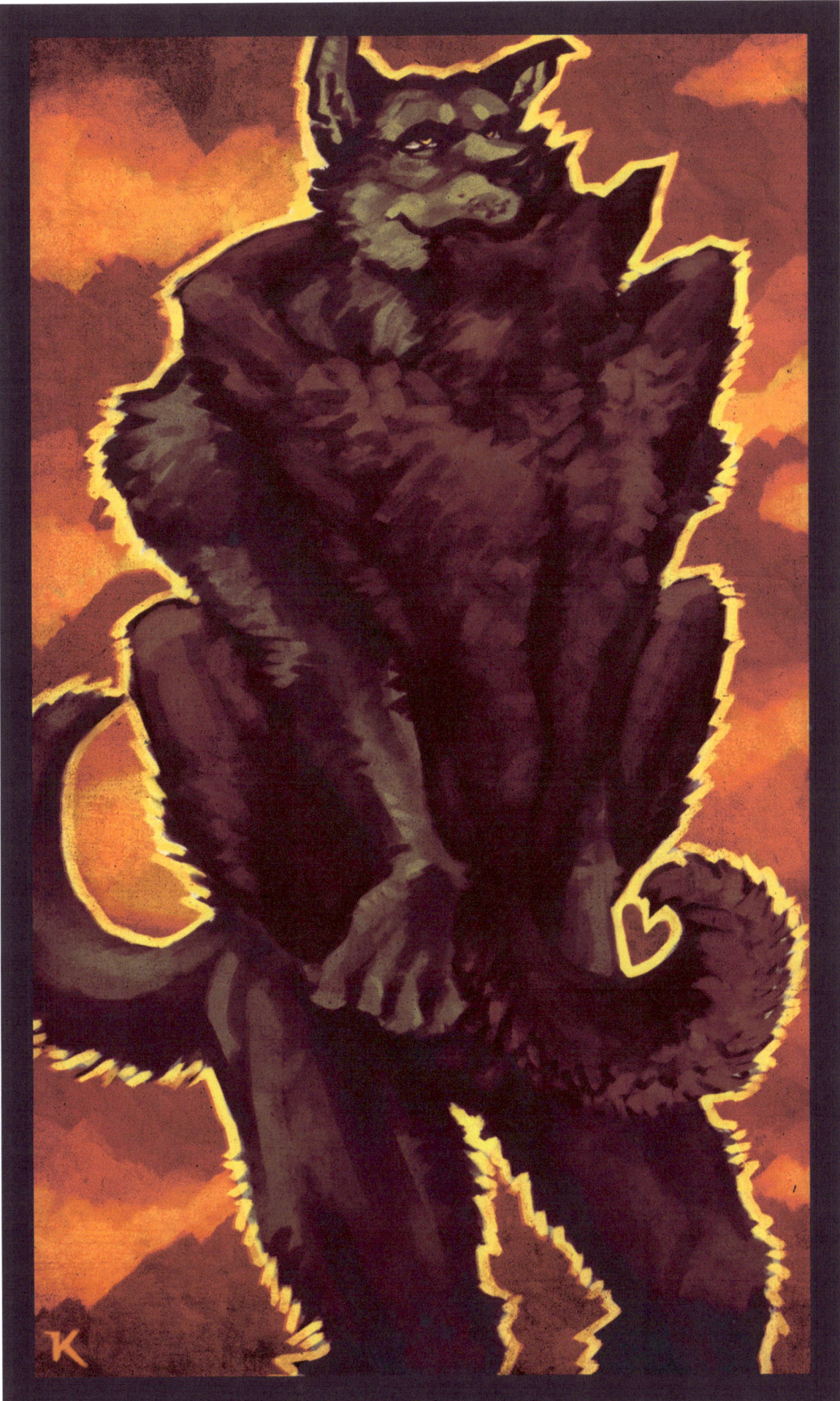

It's insanely easy to make your own brushes in Photoshop. There's a tool for every job and vice versa—if you don't have the right brush for your image, make it!

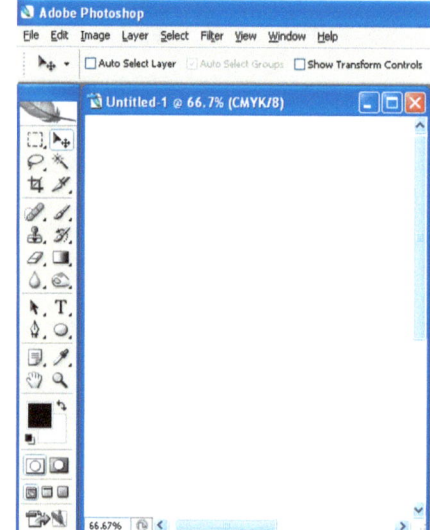

Start with a blank canvas at least as big as the new brush you want to make.

The basic process is as simple as sketching out what you want your brush to look like.

Use your existing brushes, digital photos, text, scanned patterns... Anything you like to make a mark.

We're making a brush to use with other colors later, so color doesn't matter at this stage.

Black pixels will be the opaque part of your new brush. White pixels will be transparent, and shades of gray will be as opaque as they are dark.

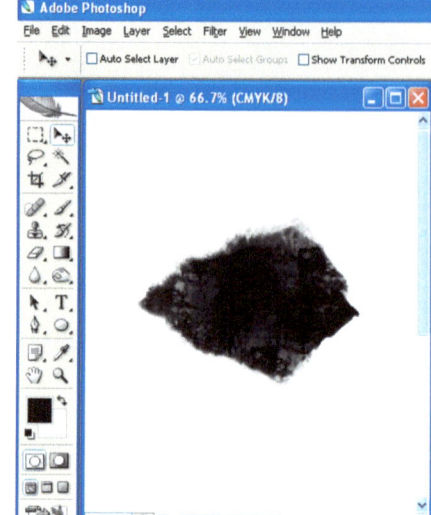

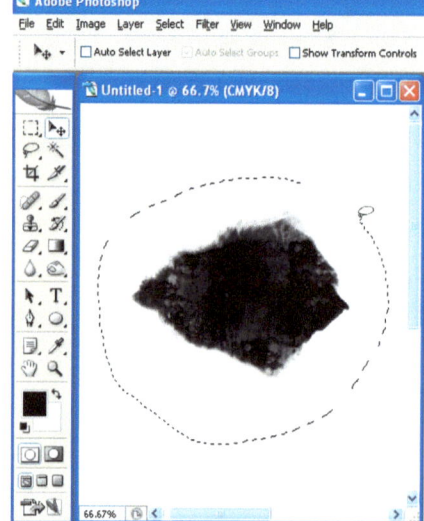

Once you're happy with your mark, use the marquee or lasso tool to create a new selection around it.

You don't have to be too exact: any white space left around the mark will be ignored automatically.

Next, go to Edit > Define Brush Preset.

Click there...

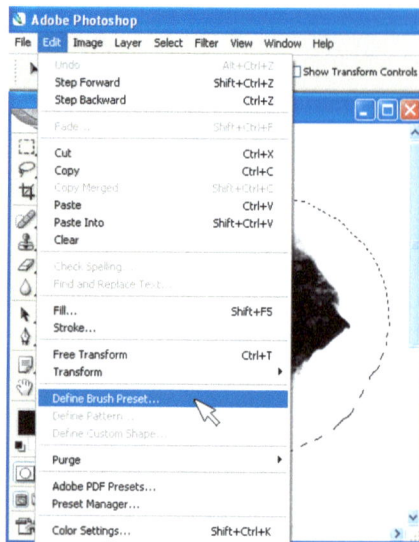

...and you'll be asked to name your new brush.

Give it a happy name.

And bingo!

There's our new brush, right at the bottom of the brush selection palette (right click on your canvas with a brush tool), ready for action!

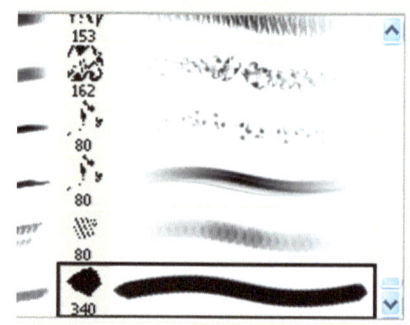

14

Aww, yeah. Just look at that chunky brush go!

That irregular shape gives it a different profile depending on which direction the stroke is going, unlike Photoshop's standard set of circle brushes, which make the same mark in any direction.

Just by using a different brush, my quick sketch got a ton of texture and extra body that I would have had to put in manually with the old brushes.

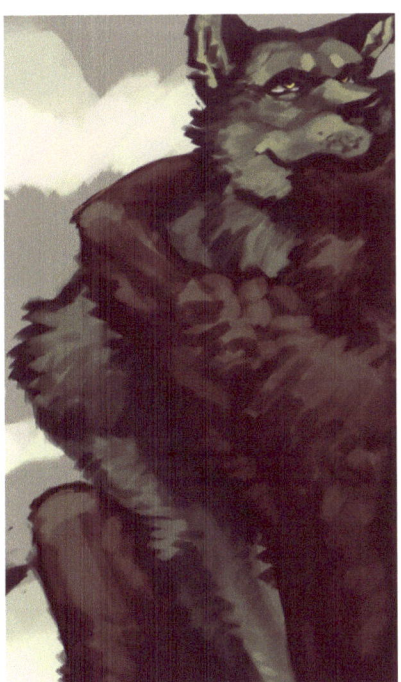

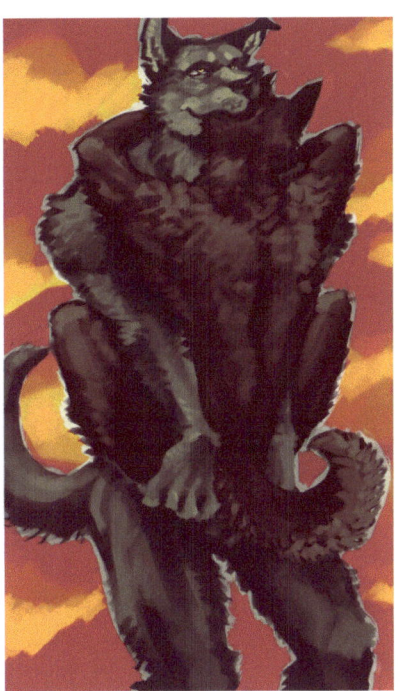

I was playing around with a hasty color overlay layer when I hit on the flaming sunset colors for the sky in the background.

I dug the effect, so it stuck. The borders of my red layer left a wonky exposed edge around the figures, though...

So I called in my new chunky brush once again!

A big, fat outline in electric yellow was just what these two needed, I'm sure.

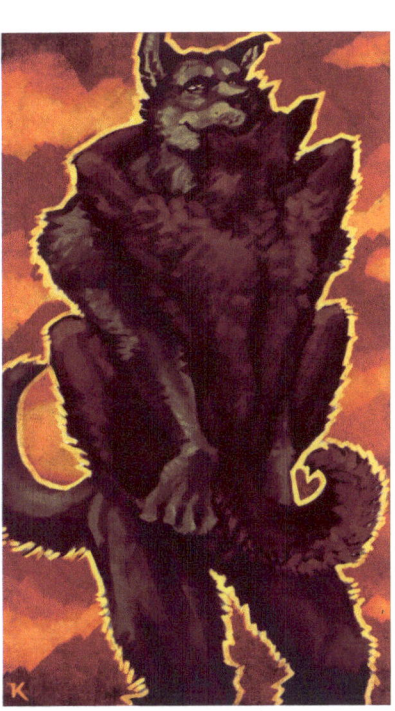

I didn't have to add much texture in the post-process phase because of how much was already in the base painting. An old paper texture and some minimal contrast adjustment later, I'm calling it done!

As a final sappy afterthought, I stuck that heart shape in to the curl of the tail.

Try custom brushes and you'll wonder how you ever got by with just the boring ol' round guys.

pl^acid rain

contrast

Pack enough visual information into an image
and it's bound to get busy (and not in the good way).
The key to making it all make sense is a strong visual hierarchy.

Figuring out what to make stand out and what to keep in the background can go a long way to preventing an image with a lot going on from becoming visual soup. It can be a good exercise to actually write down a list of the details in an image, in order of importance, and use that as a guide (then, if you're feeling daring, ask someone to look at your finished image and list what they see in the order they see it!).

So, how to give a particular detail visual weight, to call the eye's attention to it (or make sure the eye goes elsewhere)? One answer is contrast. Large/small, light/dark, detailed/sparse, jagged/smooth, crisp/blurry... There are hundreds of ways to create contrast. In this image, I kept the face and a few details like jewelry in focus while slightly blurring the rest, backlit the head with a bright, highly saturated blue to create a sharp silhouette, and lifted the body out from the background by overlaying the vines underfoot with a red texture.

Find a few ways of building contrast you like, and you're on your way to making viewers look exactly where you want them to. Just be sure to use those awesome powers for good...

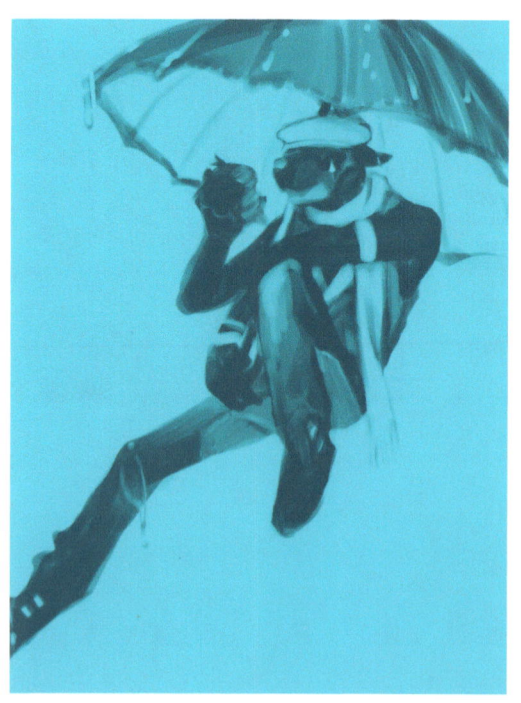 →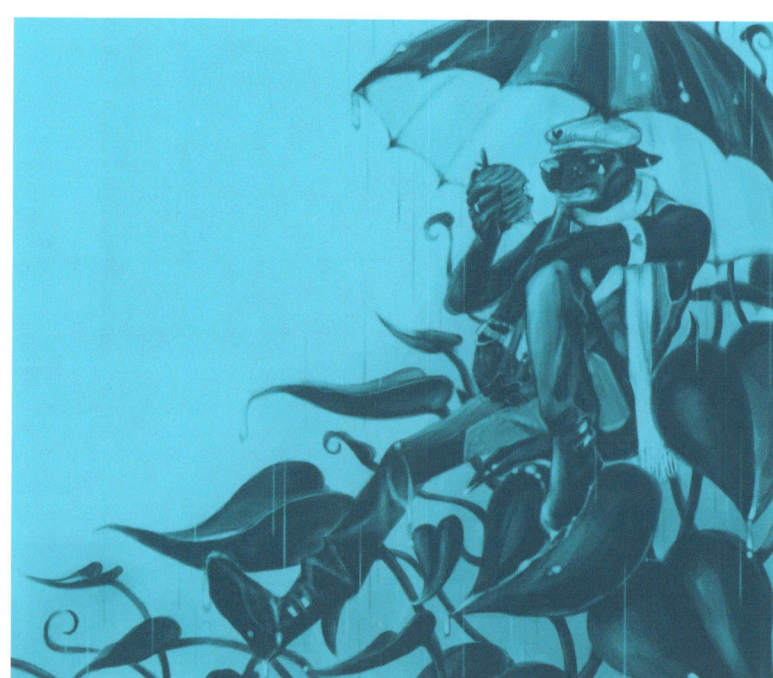

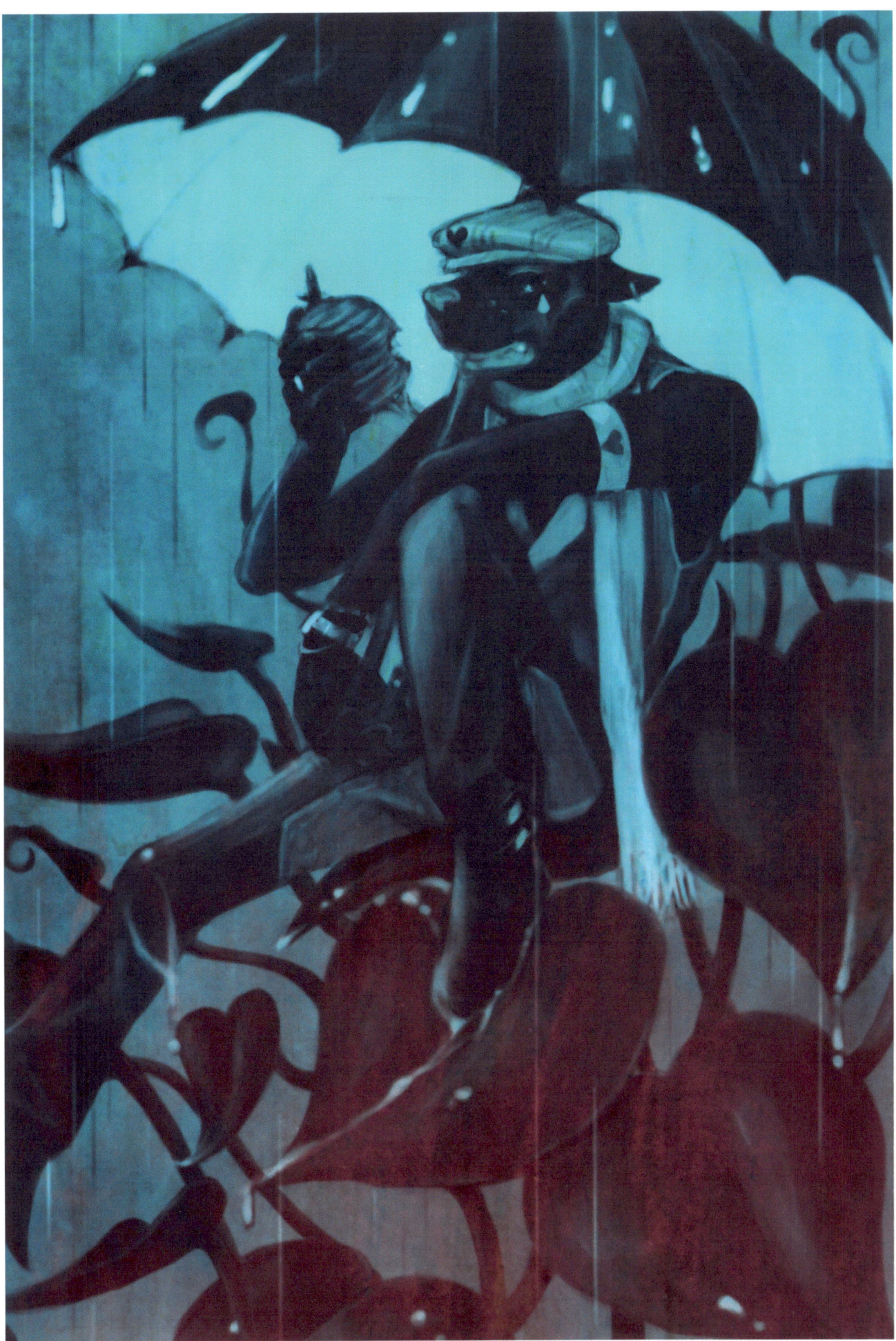

Pretty much any pair of opposites you can think up can be used to add contrast to an image. Whatever the difference, they'll help delineate one thing from the next to the eye.

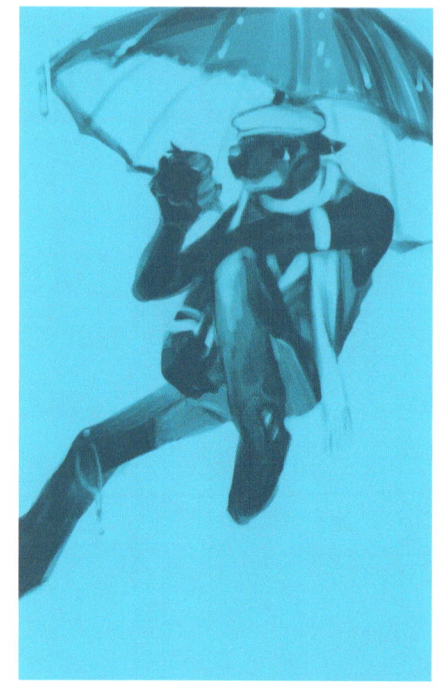

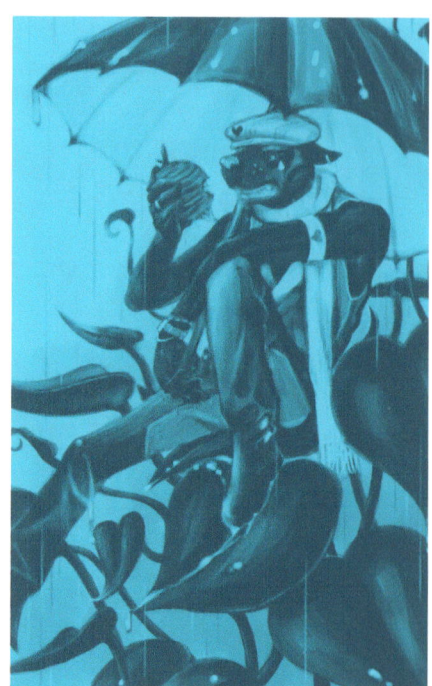

Things start off again with the basic sketch, made by hopping back and forth between the active foreground and background colors while blocking in the major forms.

That continued as I added in more detail, painted in a leafy bit of background, and shaded some until I wound up here—the finished underpainting.

Because it's only a two-tone image, and both tones blue at that, it's a relatively low-contrast image at this point.

The brightness and saturation of that lighter blue is about the only thing setting things apart now, and some of the darker and mid-tone areas are muddled.

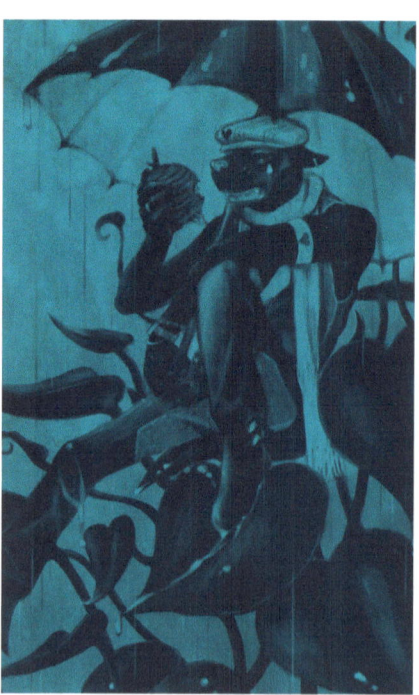

Originally, the image was comprised of light and mid-range values, with no really rich dark tones.

Adding a texture layer set to Multiply again makes everything under it darker. That doesn't solve my contrast problem for the moment, but it pushes the previously wimpy darks into ranges respectable for a rainy day scene.

Now, I can go back in and add new highlights that bring back that bright, electric blue from before, and have a dark, middle, *and* light range.

This is wood.

Wood is one of my texture files. Today, he's going to do something a little unpredictable. At the very least, I didn't see it coming.

I stick this on top of my image and set the blending mode to Pin Light, which simulates the effect of a pinhole camera, and...

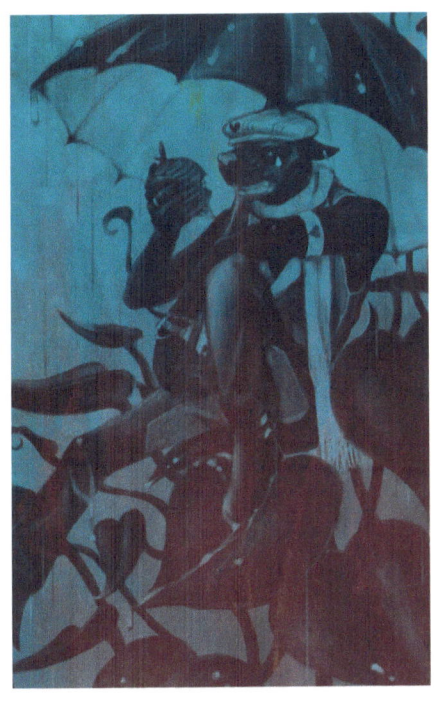

This happens!

Wow, it turned red.

Well, looking back at the original file, it was a little tough to see where the dude stopped and the vines he's sitting on began.

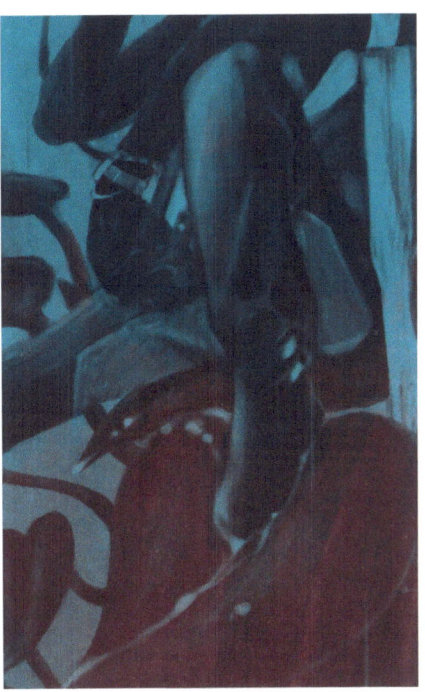

So I selectively erase away at my red texture layer where it overlaps his body.

I keep pen pressure light, as I'm not looking to erase the red completely. I want to avoid making the boundary *too* jarring.

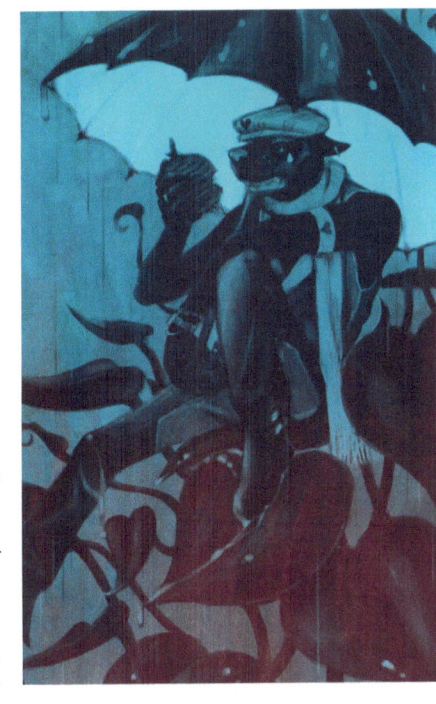

Now that I've got color working as contrast, it's time to stick that electric blue back in.

The lining of the umbrella has one of the most interesting shapes in this image, and in particular it surrounds the head and onion, two major details, so I decided to stick the light blue there.

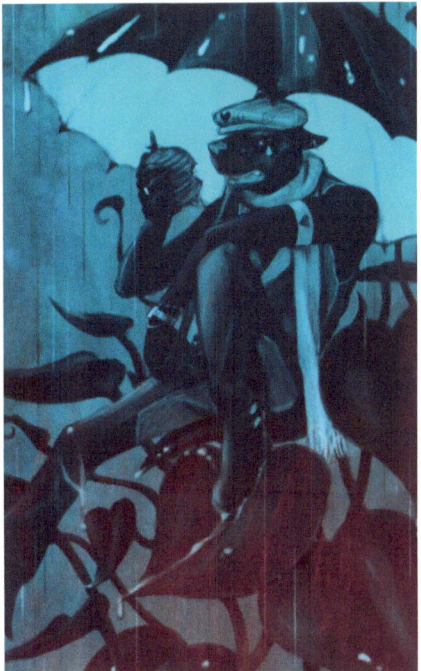

Color: check.
Value and saturation: check.

In order to rack up one more bit of contrast to really call the viewer's attention to the figure, I performed a Gaussian Blur on the image (Filter > Blur > Gaussian Blur), which takes everything out of focus.

Then, using the history brush, I painted the key detail areas back into focus.

Adding so much contrast that everything becomes uniformly different kinda defeats the purpose.

texxy

texture

Also known as the instantly un-boring layer.
Welcome to my personal best friend.

A painting will often have all of its elements present after the initial sketching and cleanup, and all that remains is going through and adding hour after hour of tiny details to give it the look and feel of being truly finished. A lot of that detail, though, is just a matter of adding fine, controlled bits of information to contrast with the broad coarseness of the basic painting structure. That means that, to an extent, *any* detail will do the trick.

Which leaves you with a choice. Either you can paint them all in by hand the old fashioned way, or you can cheat. By overlaying one or more texture files on top of your basic painting, you can instantly push it along towards appearing complete.

In this case, I threw a pair of large texture images over my paint sketch—a photograph of a crumbling, moss-grown wall, and a scan of some grainy, tarnished paper—and voilà! Experimenting with Photoshop's various layer blending modes can yield an endless variety of visual effects, even from a limited library of texture files. That said, this can be a great excuse to start carrying a camera around on random walks! In addition to being copyright free, textures you collect yourself are another way to add your own personality to the finished piece.

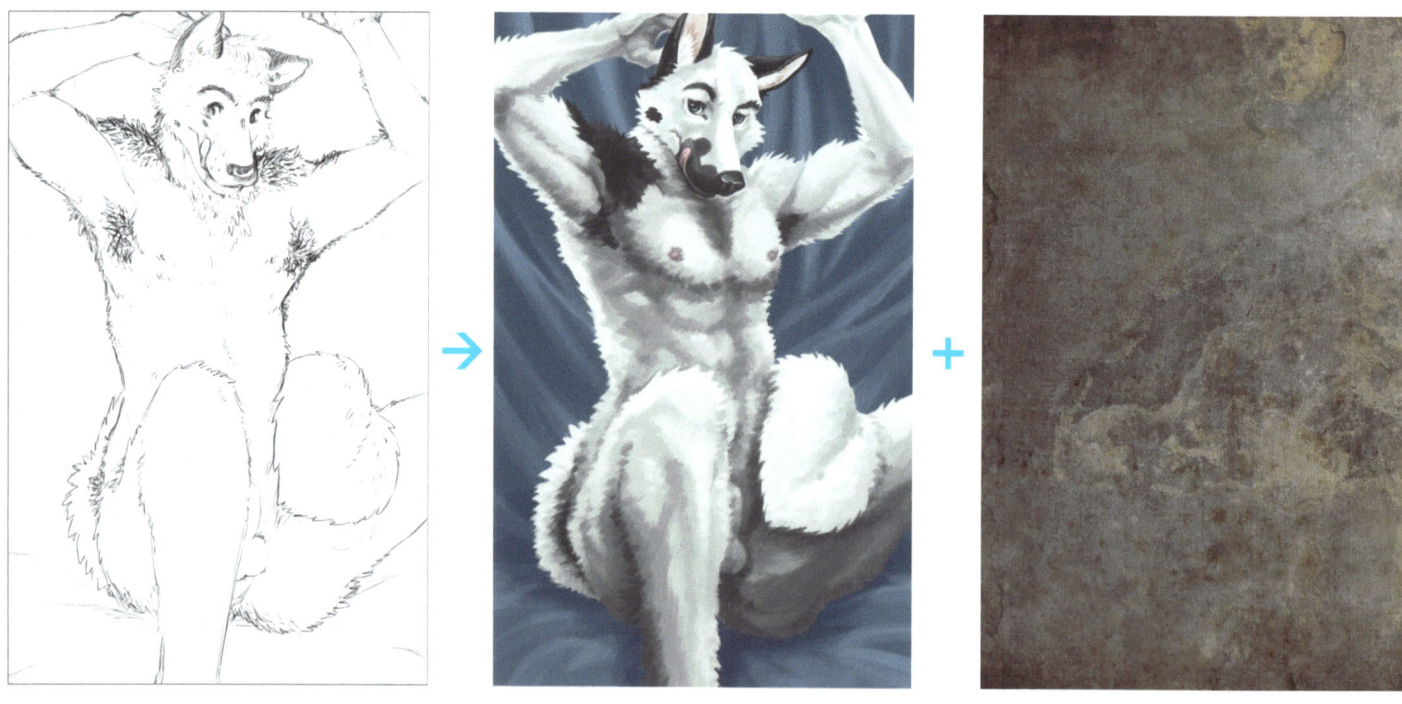

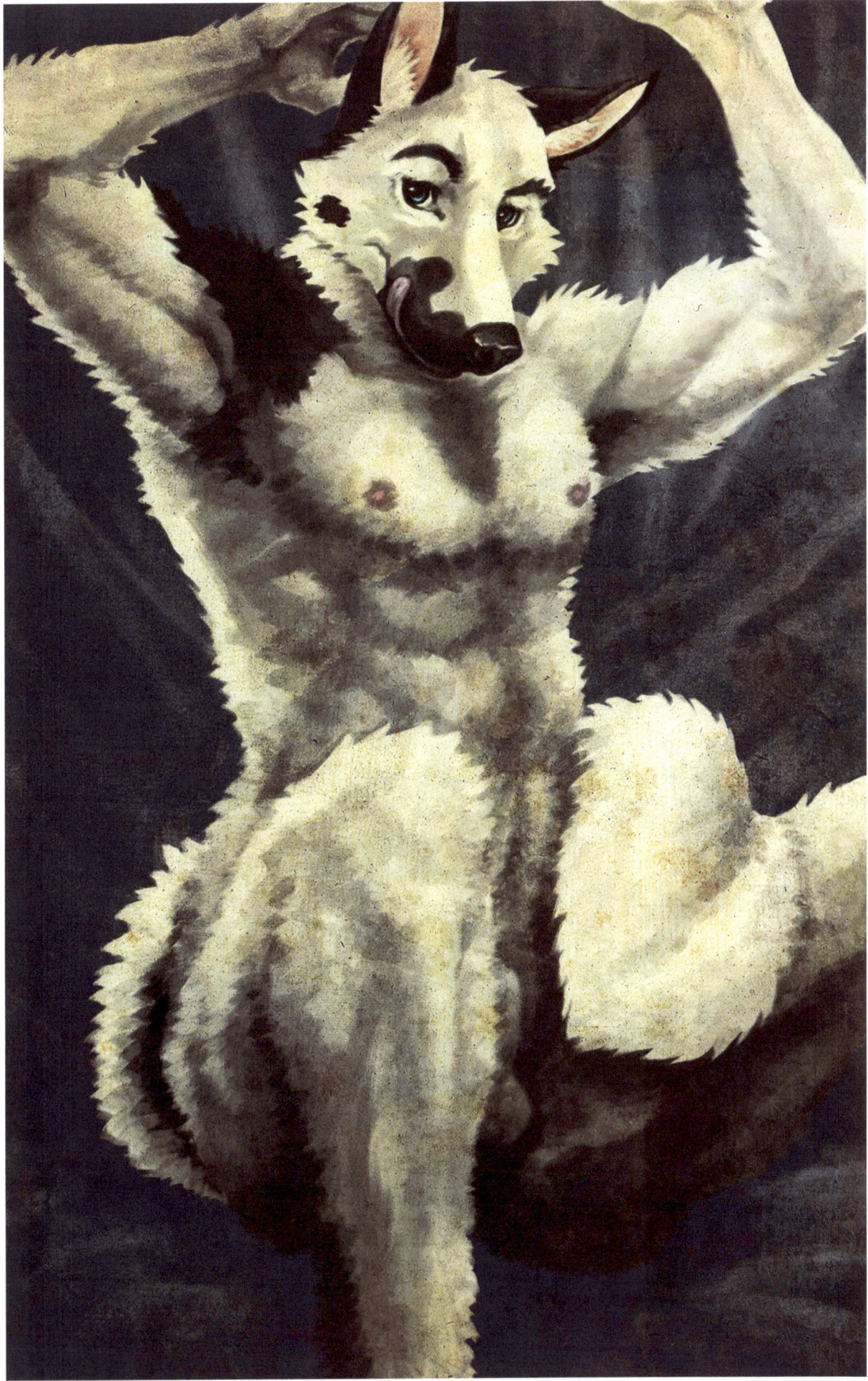

When I first discovered texture, I went a little nuts. The philosophy of "more is more" can make for some pretty intense visuals… I've calmed down a bit.

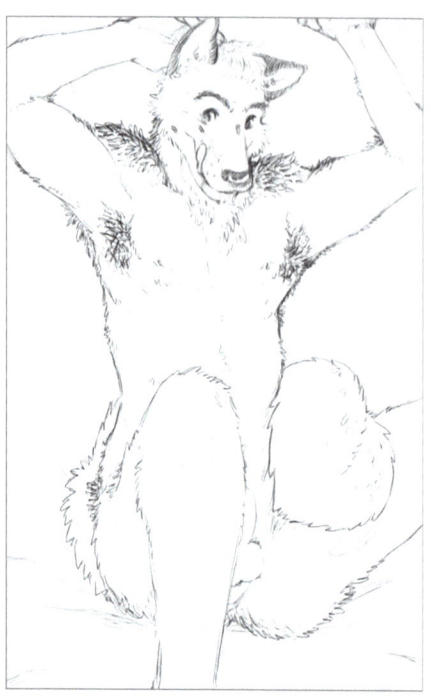

You can tell this one started from an older sketch that I decided to come back to: there are actually lines!

It was a flattened image, so to start, I double-clicked on the *Background* layer to make it an adjustable layer, which I named "lines."

Again, clearly naming your layers can be incredibly helpful down the line when you have twenty of them and forget which one has the nose…

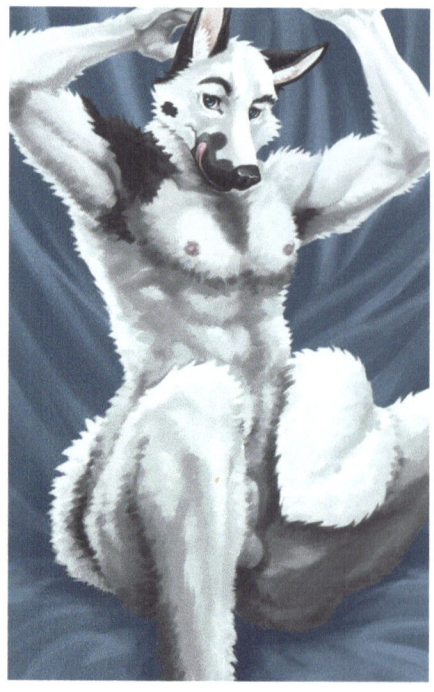

After setting my lines layer to Multiply, I made a new layer underneath it for the background, and filled it with a neutral medium blue tone.

On another layer atop that one, I start using whites and greys to carve out the figure.

Once my underpainting is done, I'm ready to hit it with some texture!

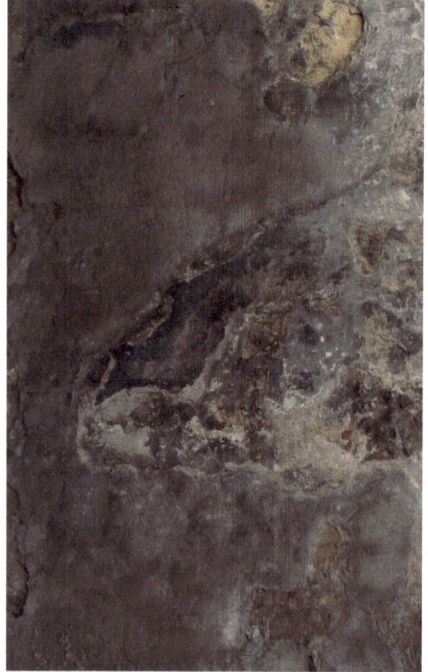

Taking photographs of walls may get you some funny looks, but it's an awesome way to build up a texture library. High-res, copyright-free textures are also available online, but be careful not to assume that everything you find is free to use. If you're not sure, don't use it!

Legal concerns aside, I put this layer on top of everything, and set the blending mode to Overlay. That mode treats the layer as sort of tinted transparent overlay which will add in color and increase the contrast by brightening the highlights and deepening shadows.

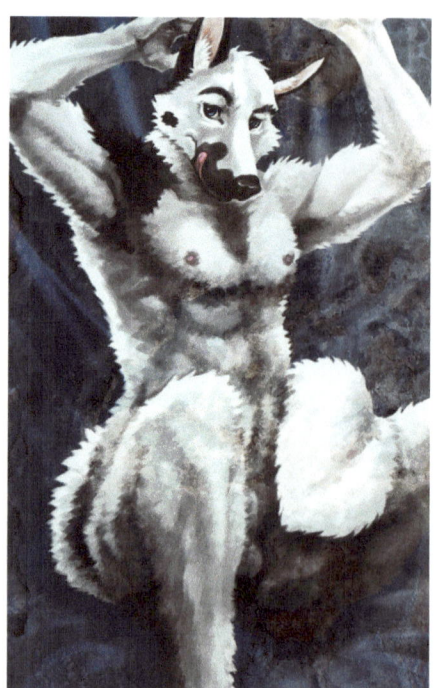

This is the immediate result.

I'm liking the details that it added, but the contrast is a little stark, and the texture is a bit too heavy overall.

22

The texture can be selectively faded back by lowering the layer's opacity. Make sure you're on the right layer, then use the sliding dialogue box in the upper right-hand corner of the layers palette to set the opacity to the desired level.

For this guy, I felt that around 50% was just right. At half strength, the wall texture does its thing without distracting from the image underneath it.

Muuuch better.

A little bit of texture can make it seem like you worked a lot harder than you did, but add too much and it can be overpowering, making all the effort you *did* put in on the piece a waste.

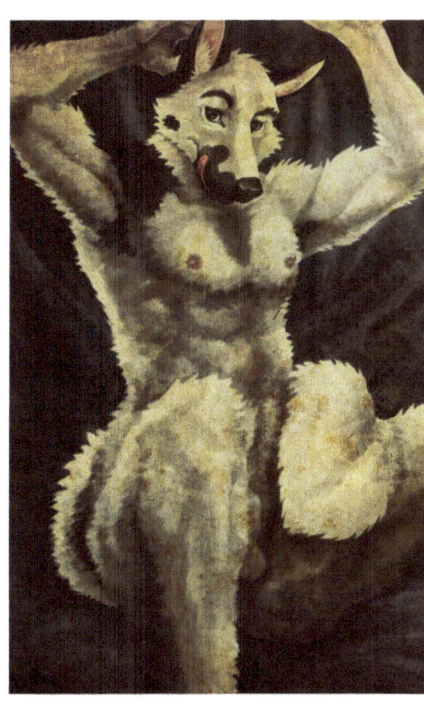

With the first texture layer all set up, I'm ready for another one! This time, I took a scan of some old, grungy paper and placed it on top of the layer stack set to Linear Burn, which will supercharge your shadows and infuse them with a lot of saturated color.

Again, the texture layer was too potent at maximum strength, so I scaled it down to about 65% opacity, which was enough to leave some grit and warm, yellowy color without totally overloading the eyes.

Be careful: this texture stuff is like crack cocaine. Brace yourself for addiction.

milk bath
ideation

We all hit dry spells.
The trick is not letting them stop you.

There are generally two courses of action available when you've run into a wall. One is to wait it out. Take a break, go for a walk, read a book, socialize. Eventually, whatever block was precluding you from getting into the Zone will melt away, you'll be infused with inspiration and new purpose, and even you will be powerless to stop the inexorable creative flood from pouring out.

For the stumped artist who needs relief *now*, however, that isn't always an option. Whether you're on a tight deadline or just feeling impatient, the alternative to going the long way around a wall is to break through it using brute force. Draw and draw and draw until *some*thing clicks, then run with it like you stole it.

One option for coming up with possible images (*ideating,* in art jargon) is to throw down random shapes and lines and let something materialize on its own. Forget about driving for a minute, sit back, and let the paint tell you where to go next. It's hit or miss, but doesn't require any fancy ideas beforehand, making it ideal for getting un-stumped.

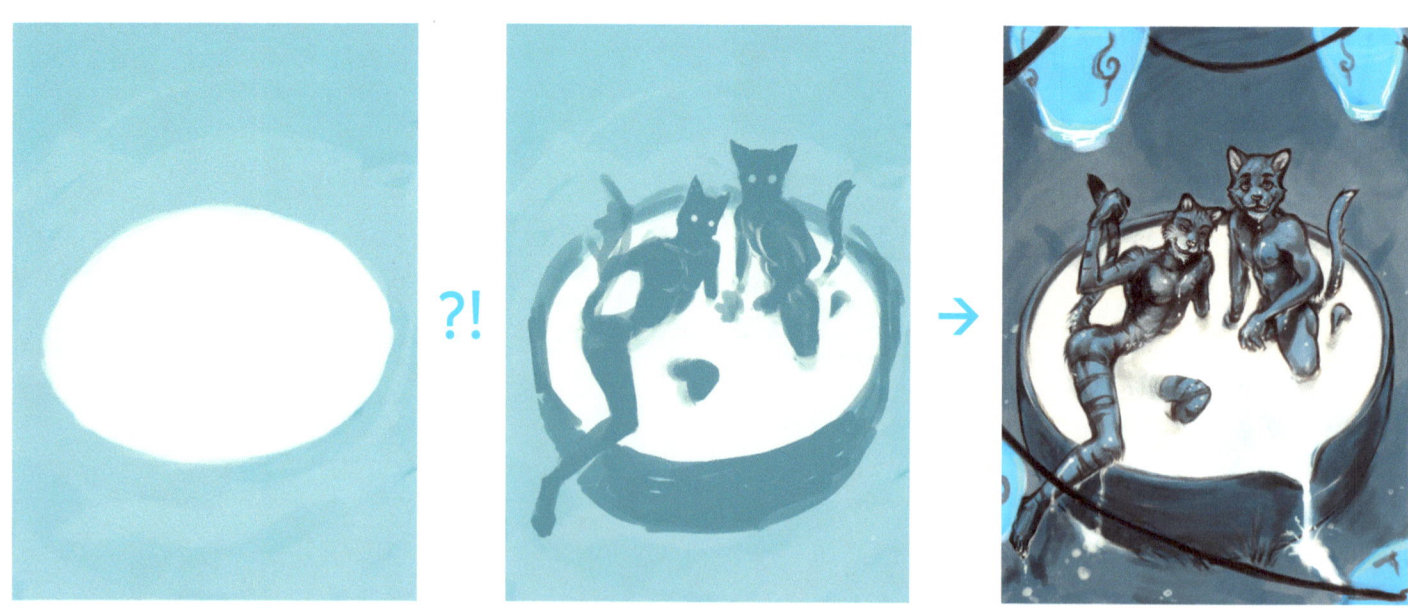

Sometimes a milky white blob can be enough to make you think of a saucer of cream, which makes you think of cats, which makes you think of I don't even want to know what...

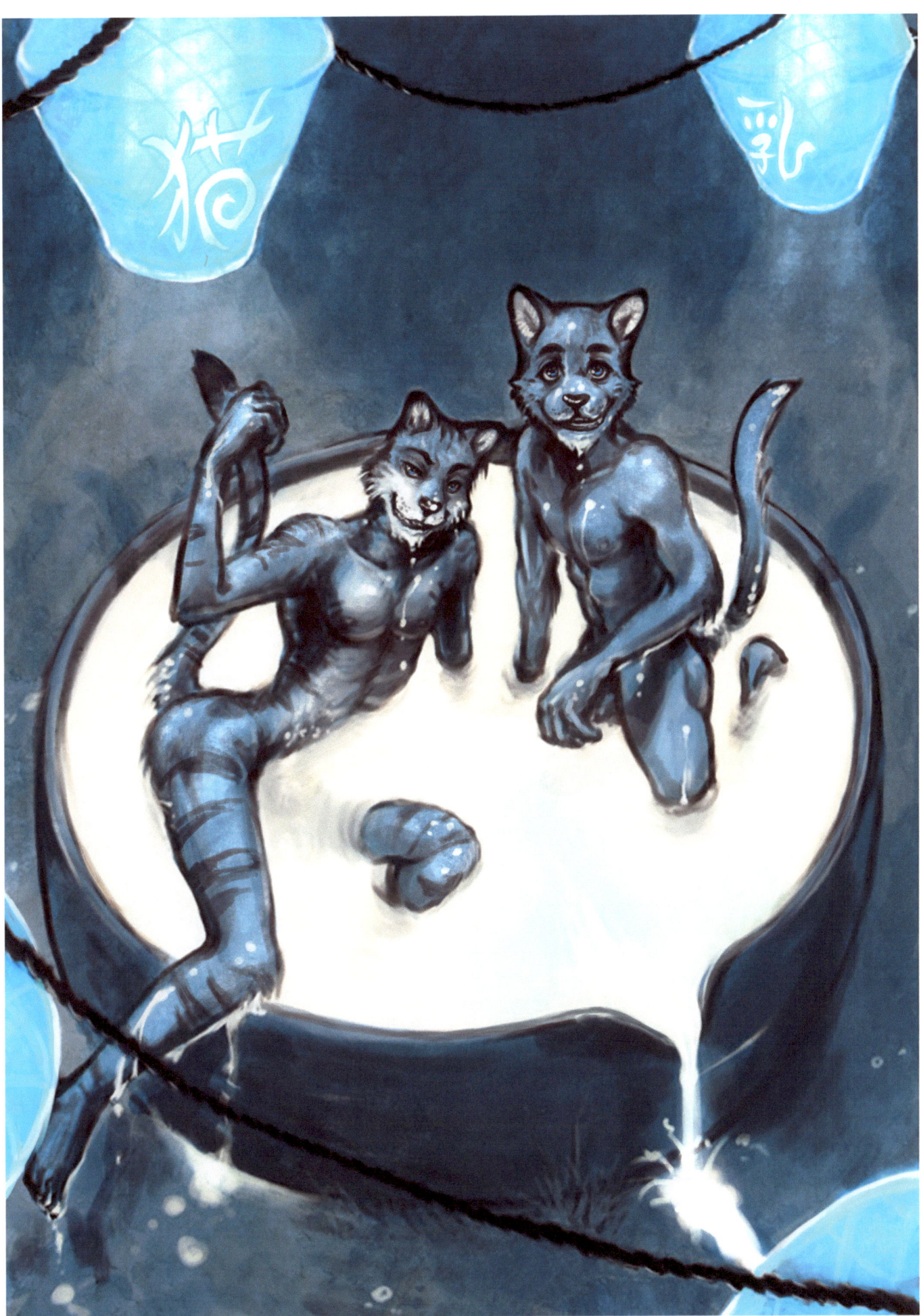

When you want your neon-lit highlights to really go atomic and your shadows to go all the way to 11, the dodge & burn tools can help you out.

I started out simple this time. One thing to keep in mind when beginning an image is that the colors you choose here will determine the range of values you can get later.

If you start with straight white or black off the bat, you won't be able to go any lighter or darker later on.

I recommend choosing a mid-tone background, and that you save your lightest lights and darkest darks for the end, when you know the full range of your piece's values.

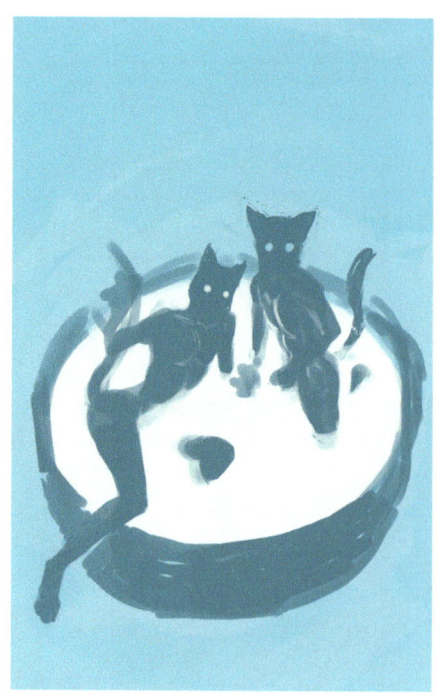

Using a dark color, a mid-tone, and a light color to sketch keeps everything easy to see as I go.

The colors are subject to change as the piece develops, but it never hurts to start with a clear palette.

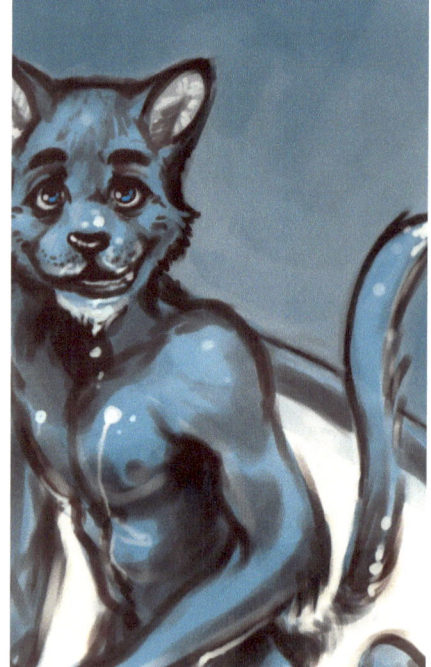

Blue and orange are *complementary* colors, which is to say opposites. That means that they produce a lot of contrast when sitting next to each other, and mix together to form a neutral tone. The more saturated the colors, the stronger the effect.

The color of the cream and the brown I'm using for lines are both close relatives in the orange family, and fairly saturated, so they're popping against the blue nicely.

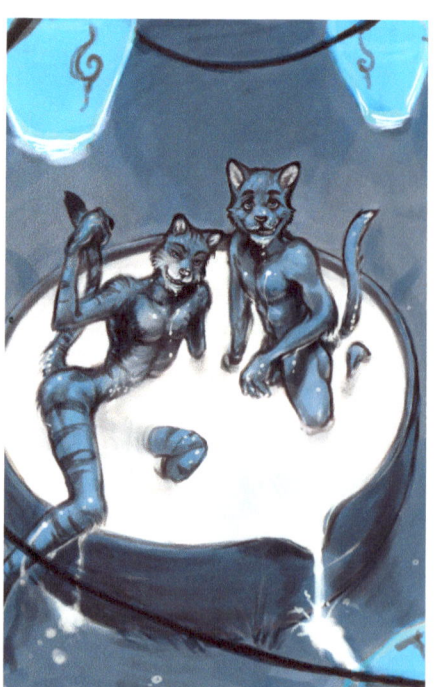

That about takes care of my underpainting.

It's a bit rough, but the lighting and texture I'm about to put over it will help with that, and I want to leave some of the liveliness of my sketched lines intact.

I'm ready to start dodging and burning.

The dodge & burn tools are located together in the tools palette—just click and hold on the icon to bring up the dialogue shown here.

Dodge makes things brighter, burn makes them darker.

This is also the home of the sponge tool, which is used to selectively increase or decrease color saturation.

The pull-down dialogue box at the top (highlighted here in orange) lets you select the range of values affected by the dodge & burn tools.

For now, I want to amp up my highlights, so I've chosen the dodge tool, and set the range to Highlights.

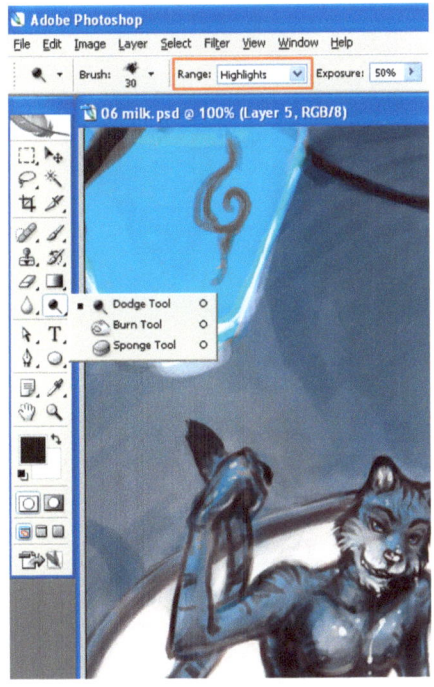

Next, I just choose a scratchy brush with a nice texture and start dodging away.

The dodge & burn tools tend to be *extremely* potent. You'll want to go easy on the pressure if you're using a tablet, or set the exposure level down from 100% (see the dialogue box directly to the right of the range setting pictured to the left).

Another handy method that I use regardless of which tool I'm using is the Fade option. Go to Edit > Fade to bring up a little dialogue box that lets you reduce the opacity of your last action on a sliding scale from 0 to 100%.

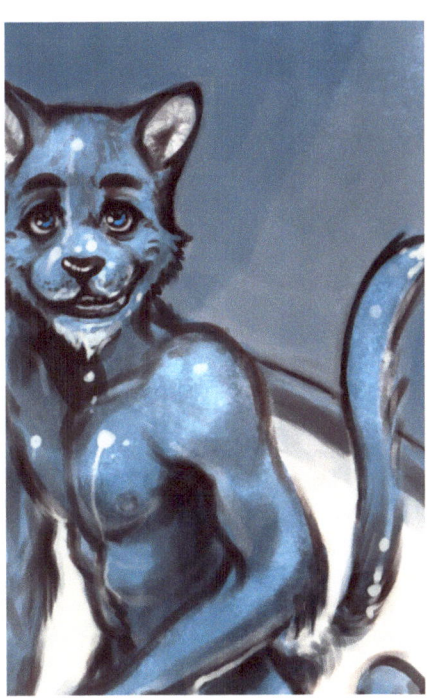

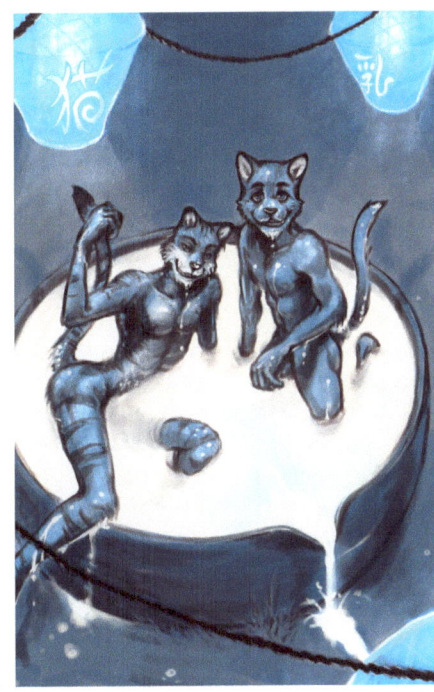

Post-dodge, those lamps are really looking neon, and the highlights on the kitties are brighter than white!

Now the shadows need some of the love...

By using the burn tool, set to affect the Shadows, my mid-tones take a quick nose-dive towards black, yielding a rich, hyper-saturated greenish blue.

Keeping the figures mostly un-burned prevents their internal contrast from going too crazy, while increasing their contrast against the background, lifting them up off the page.

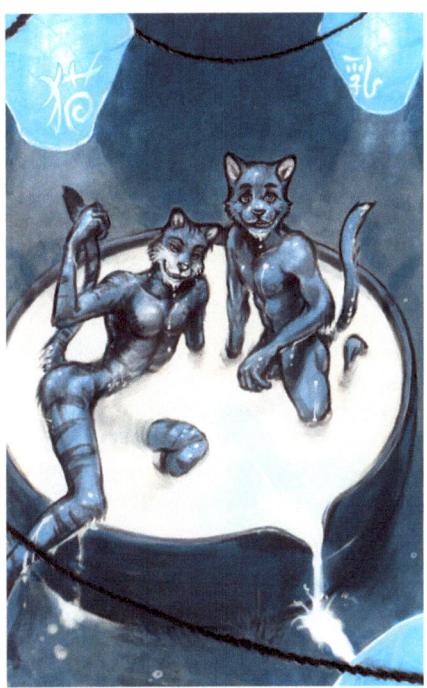

Remember—these are for adjusting, not painting. Trust me, your colors will go kinda gross.

curtains!
composition

What makes an image feel right?
No, seriously, I'm asking.

Well, the answer is a collection of things. Perspective and proportion, use of color... The list goes on. The bedrock of any solid image is its construction on the canvas—its composition. At its core, composition is an organizational thing; the placement of shapes, lines, and blank space within the image. For reasons that likely lie somewhere between cultural preferences and human eye anatomy, some compositions feel more comfortable than others to view.

In some ways, an image can be likened to music. Is it sparse and minimalist, with just a few key accents to make its point, or is it a cacophony of tightly-packed chords and complex melodies? One isn't any better or worse than the next, but they convey different moods, which should be consciously matched (or mismatched) to suit the content of the image.

A major part of visual composition is the way the eye flows over the image. The less you force the eye to work in ways it doesn't naturally, the more comfortable the composition will be to view. That can mean using strong diagonals in your piece (imagine key details forming a line across the page that the eye can easily follow), obeying the *rule of thirds* (center the action around a horizontal one- or two-thirds up the canvas), and plenty of open space.

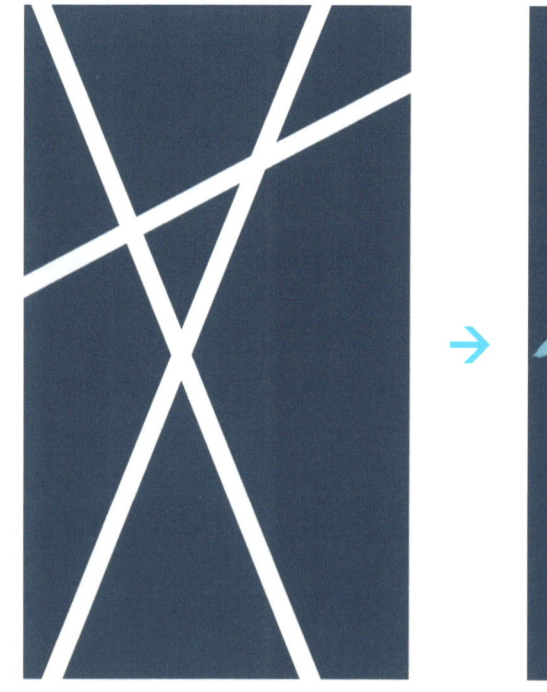 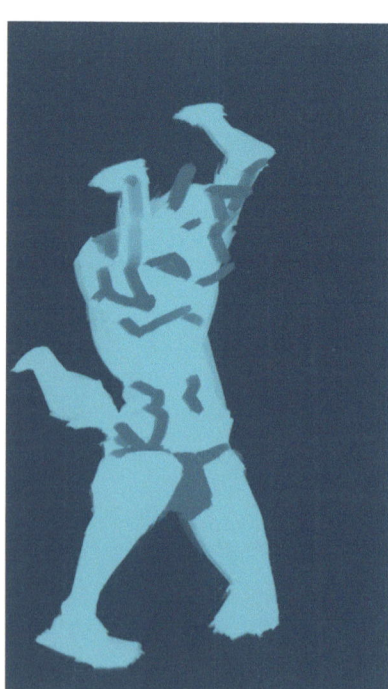 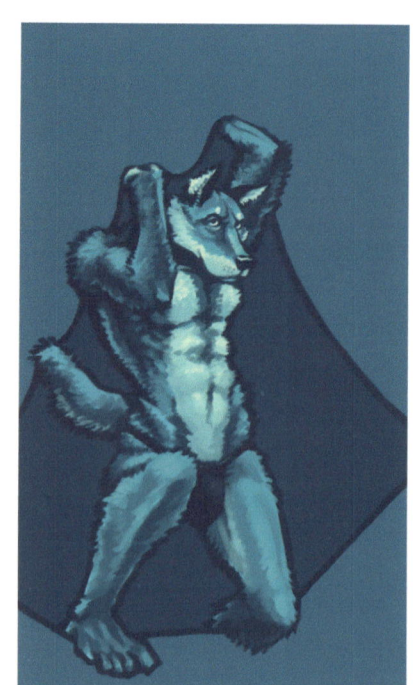

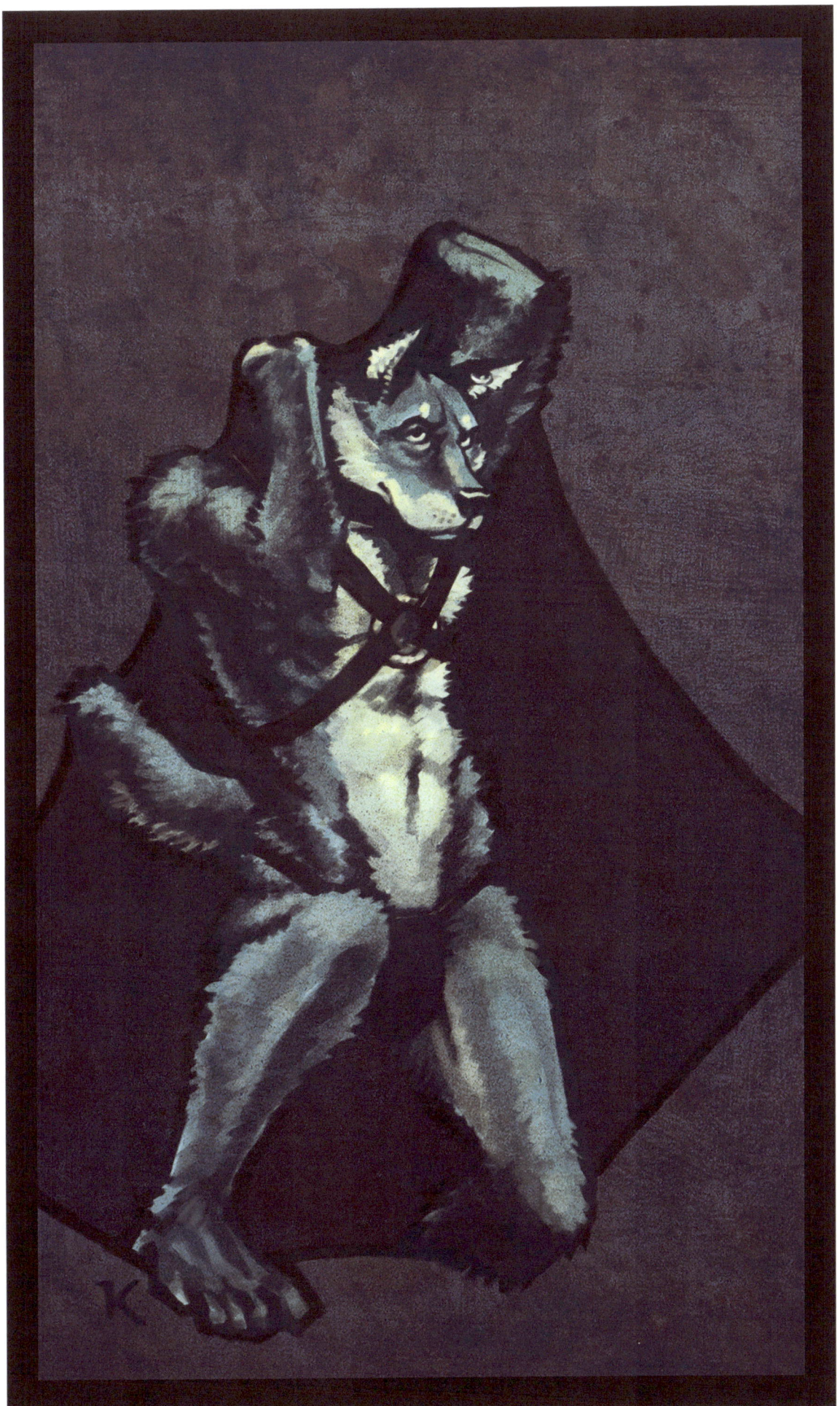

Okay, I know what you're thinking... "Charts? *Graphs?!*" Hear me out. Most of it is common sense, but thinking about it when you draw can make a big difference.

So, most of the lighter colored blue space, by straight percentage, is contained in the body of the huge arrow, and most of *that* is in the upper half of the image.

So why does everybody focus on the tiny circle at the very bottom? The answer is obvious: because there are arrows pointing at it.

Well, what you might not stop to think about is that shapes that are a lot less obvious than arrows can still point attention in different directions.

Take this case.

Uniform circles and squares here—no big arrows to point the way. Still, the eye moves to the third circle from the bottom. It's no bigger or brighter than the others, but it pulls you in the hardest.

Again, the reason is obvious, but sometimes it's easy to forget the obvious things.

As the point of intersection between two suggested lines, that circle is smack in the middle of a giant X.

Details in a picture can form similar suggested lines, and the eye will always be drawn to their intersections. Make sure to park the detail you want people to look at in that spot!

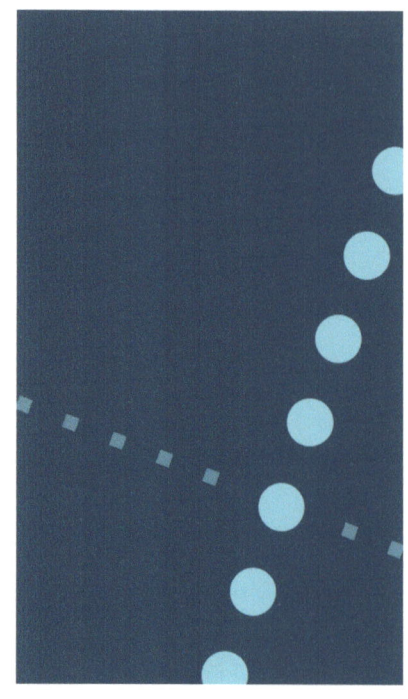

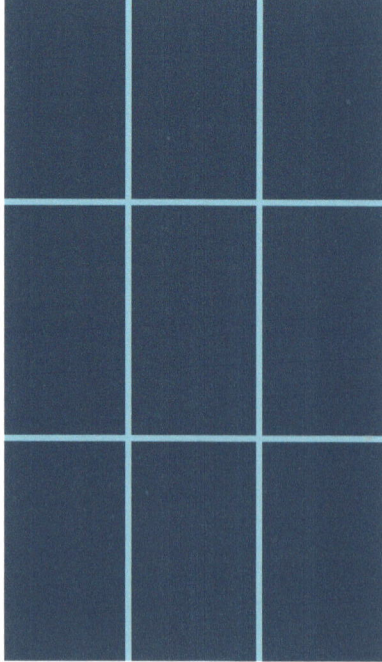

Putting the focus of your image right in the middle will call attention to it, but it can also make a composition feel heavy and lifeless.

For a more dramatic framing, use the *rule of thirds*.

Here I've divided the canvas into even thirds vertically and horizontally. By aligning the key line(s) of your image to one of those guides (a standing person along one of the verticals, for example, or the horizon line along one of the horizontals), you'll add a bit of asymmetry to your piece, which will lend it movement.

Here's my basic sketch of our hero doing his best impression of Atlas.

I've drawn him over to the left of the center, just about centered over the left vertical guideline. The right third is pretty much totally empty.

Now, to be honest, I didn't actually use a grid when I painted this picture, but it's a good exercise, and a nice way of showing what was going on in my mind as I worked.

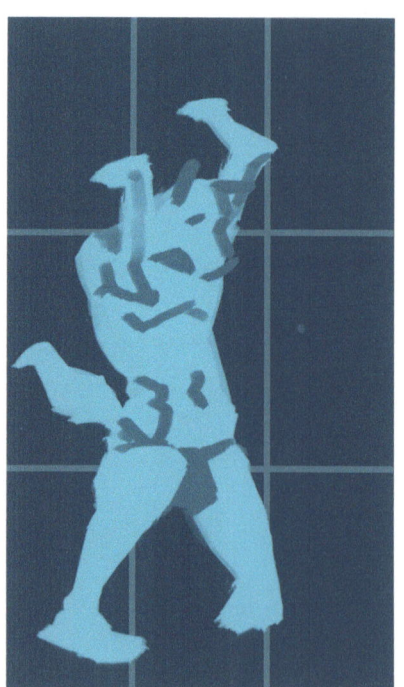

The hands, elbows, head, and shoulder form a suggested line here, and the placement of his limbs create a big X.

Posing the limbs in an X is actually an ancient concept that you see frequently in Ancient Greek sculpture and the like.

The technical term for his pose is *chiastic contraposto*, where *chiastic* comes from the Greek letter *chi,* or *X.*

Contraposto refers to the line of the shoulders tilting opposite ("*contra*") the line of the hips, which makes for some sexy curves!

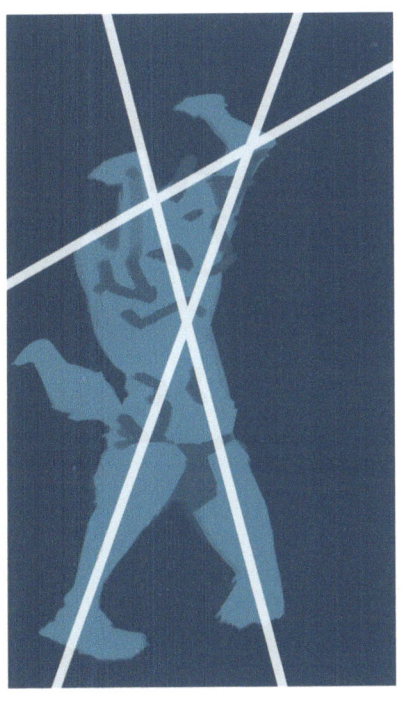

Enough with the charts and graphs and jargon already!

Here, I've got most of the basics down. Now to tweak the colors, add some contrast, and give it some texture!

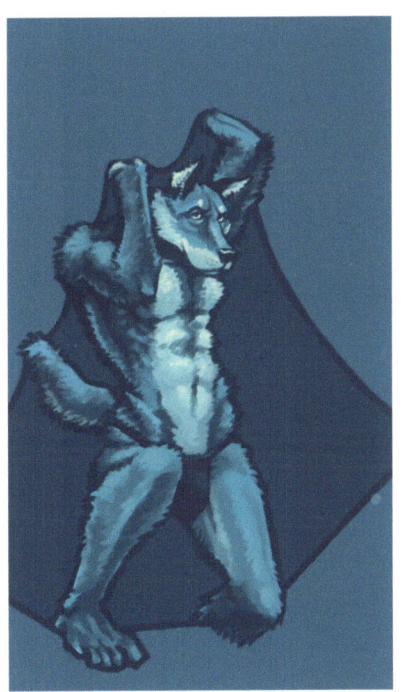

I gave him a leather harness that crosses at the solar plexus, right where the lines shown above intersect.

His shin, hamstring, and jock are forming another cross to strategically call attention to the area at their intersection.

X marks the spot!

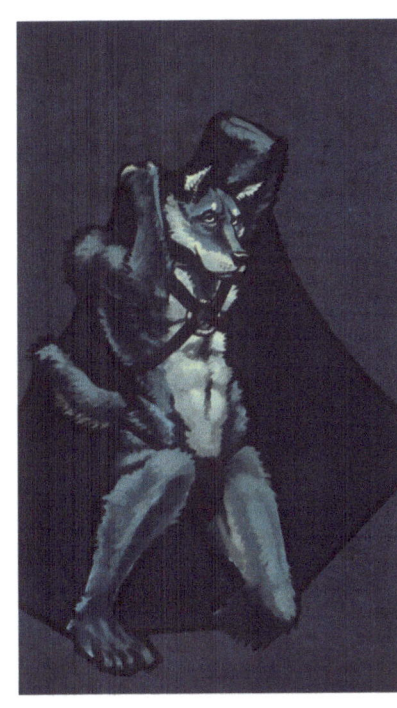

With a little playing around, this one's all done!

I'm not sure if it's all the X's or the situation he finds himself in, but this dog seems more than a little cross.

...Sorry. I had to say it.

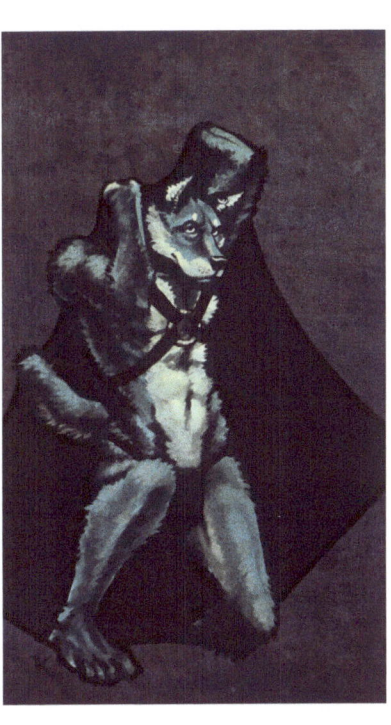

The crotch is a potent natural visual anchor. Handle with care!

hugs on high
design elements

The line separating illustration from graphic design gets blurrier every day.
As far as I can tell, illustrators are the ones who wear blue jeans,
while graphic designers mostly wear black.

Dropping a few crisp graphic elements into your illustration can be an interesting way to give it form, texture, and that little something extra. Here, I spiced up an otherwise empty background with a bit of pattern, texture, and graphic linework. For artists with a looser painting style like mine, the clean, formal shapes of a perfectly straight line or precise circle can provide an interesting visual contrast to the more organic shapes the brush leaves on the canvas.

In days gone by, that would have meant pulling out the compass and straightedge, but that's a bit more effort than I'm likely to muster. Luckily for me, those perfect shapes are a breeze to create using Bezier curves in Photoshop, and the graphic forms you create can then easily be painted over, erased away at, or otherwise manipulated to get them to marry with the rest of your image without sticking out *too* much.

Another great advantage of using paths is that they are infinitely scalable, meaning that you can use the shapes you create at any size later on with no sacrifice in image quality.

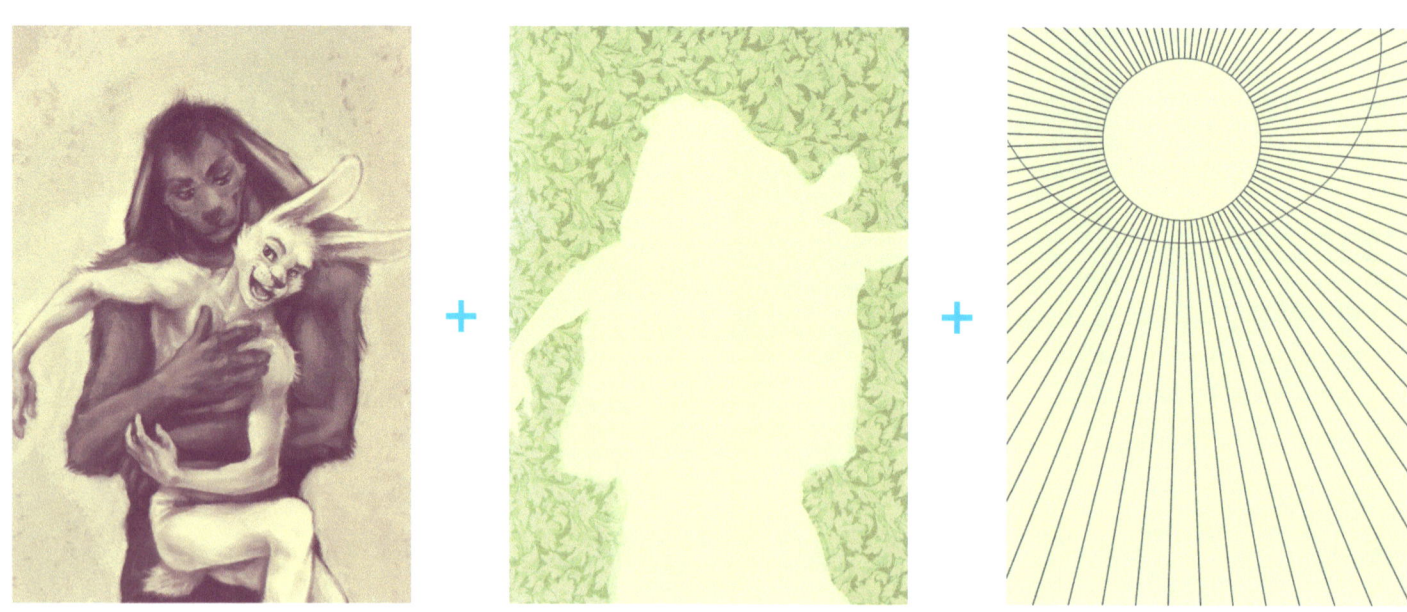

Graphics can be powerful tools in directing the eye.
The blank circle surrounded by converging lines here makes for a giant optical bull's-eye.

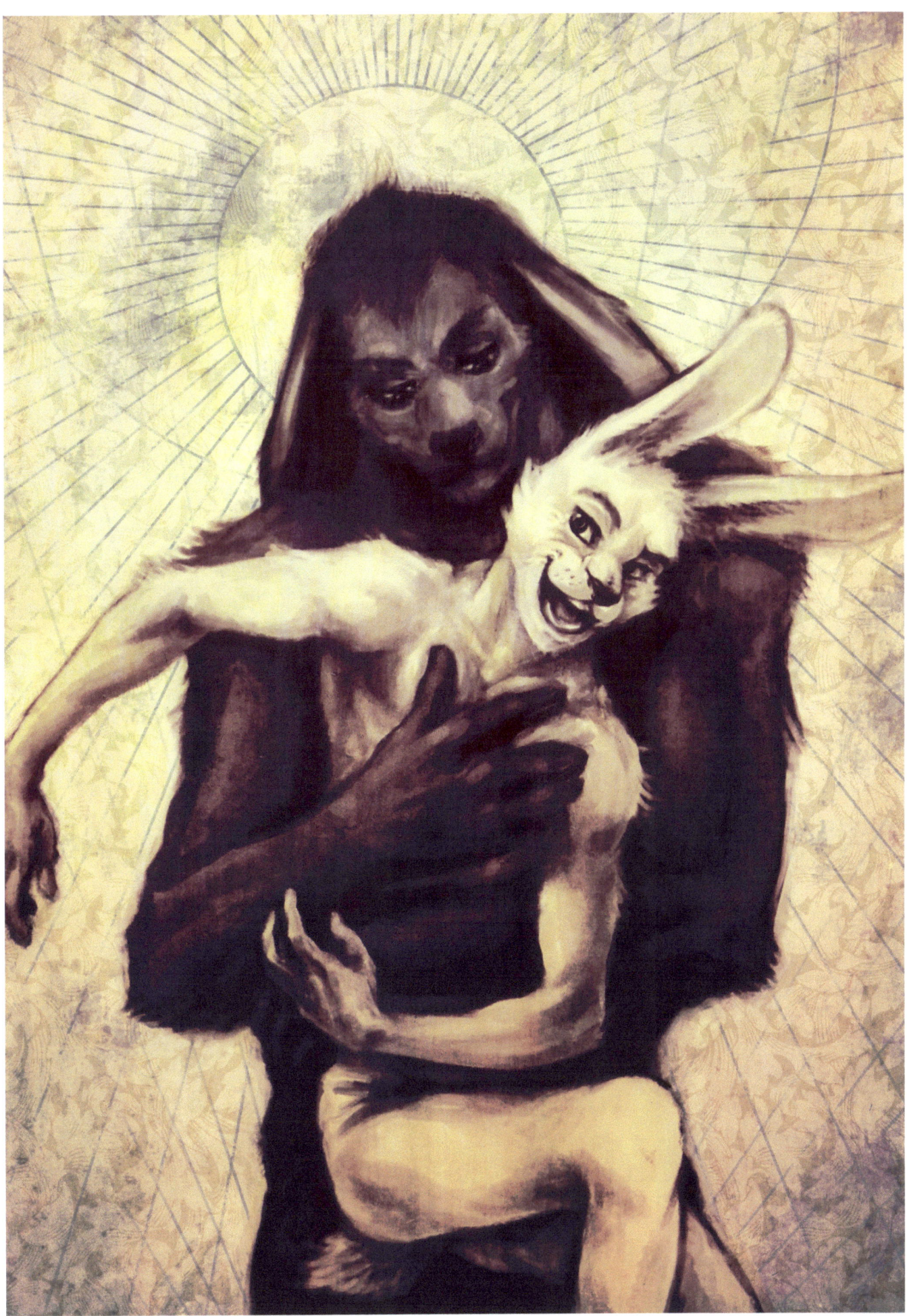

Using paths in Photoshop isn't quite as intuitive as using a brush, but with a little practice you'll be making perfect curves and board-straight lines effortlessly.

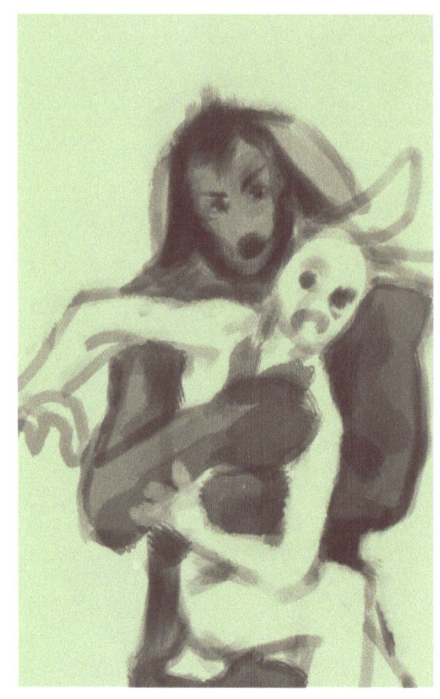

As usual, I start out with a super-quick rough sketch to block in the basic forms and tweak the pose.

Wow, that little guy doesn't seem to like that, huh?

Well, fear not, little guy—as a big proponent of consensual hugs, I'll see to it that everybody's happy by the end.

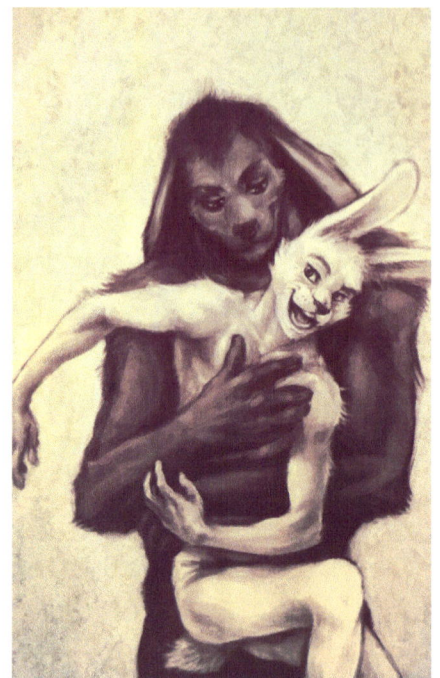

The figures are done, and I've started to add a bit of texture to the background with a brush and a light pattern set on top.

The background still feels pretty empty to me, though, so I get ready to bust out the pen and shape tools and go to town.

Next, I turn off the top layers so I have a nice, clean page to work on, then select the ellipse tool.

I want a perfect circle, so I hold down the SHIFT key while dragging the circle's boundaries to a size I'd like.

After the path is down, the direct select tool (the white arrow shown to the right) can be used to move around the little lines sticking out of the points on the path.

Those lines are called *control handles*, and are used to bend the path around the points. The direction they go determines the angle the path will follow, and their length sets the degree of influence—the longer the handle, the more they'll bend the path in their direction.

In the case of this circle, though, Photoshop already did all the work for me.

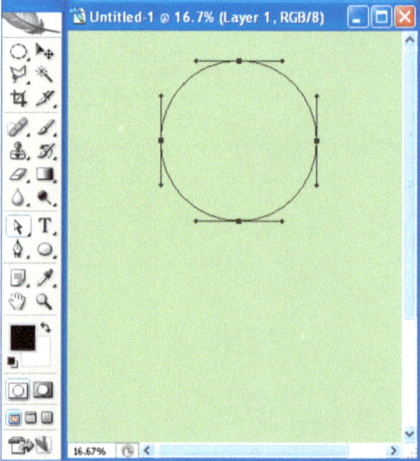

34

After making a pair of circles, I thought I'd mix it up with some radial lines to make a sort of classical iconic halo.

There are multiple methods for making radial lines, but the simplest is to draw a line (using either the line tool or a 2-point straight path made with the pen tool), copy it, paste, then rotate it into the desired position of the next spoke and paste again.

Lather, rinse, repeat. There are ways to automate the process, but let's keep it simple for now.

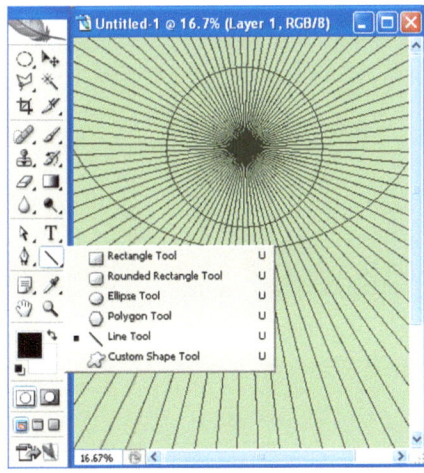

Once the path is ready, there are two things you need to check before you stroke it (and yes, that's the technical term).

First, because Photoshop will be running the brush tool along the path, we need to make sure the current brush settings and active color are what we want them to be.

Next, double-check the layer you're currently painting on. If you don't have any layers selected, you won't be able to stroke the path. In this case, I'm making an overlay, so I want to be sure I'm stroking on an empty layer.

Just click OK, and you're set!

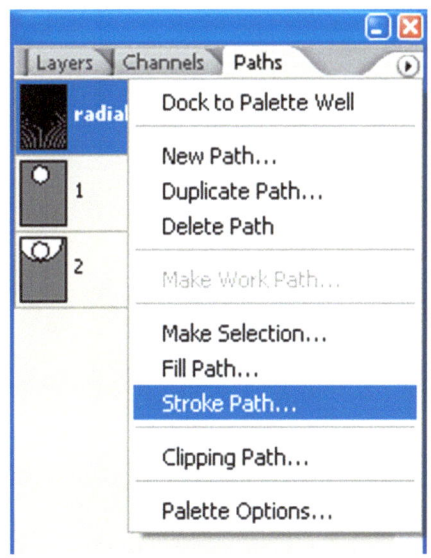

Then you just get to sit back and watch Photoshop zoom along the path, painting perfect circles and straight lines so you don't have to!

With my graphic layer done, I'm now ready to turn back on the other layers, stick this guy on top, and erase back into it with a scratchy brush to antique it a bit.

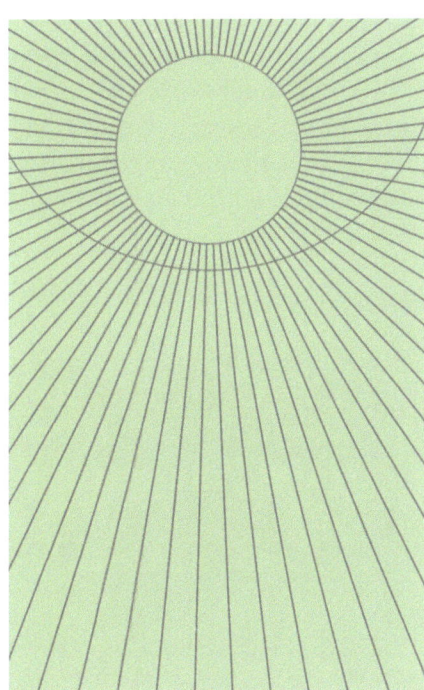

A few minor adjustments later, this one's ready to go! I like the look of the hard lines and clean forms after they've been eroded away at—that also helps marry them a bit with the messier textures in the background, and the looser organic shapes in the figures.

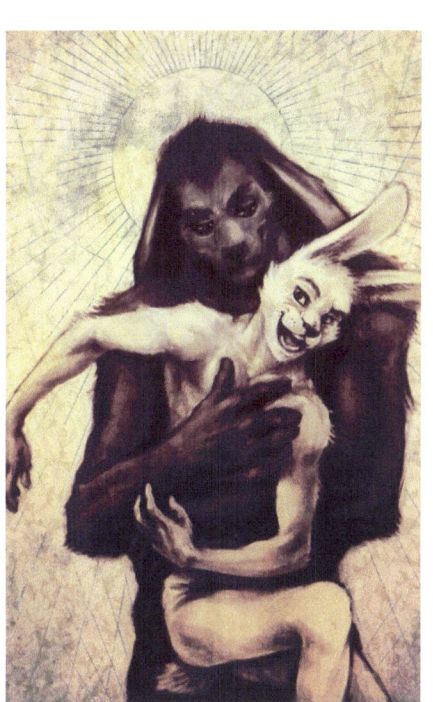

Freehand drawing a clean circle is hard enough. Doing it with a mouse? No, thanks.

35

white crusade
setting the scene

They say the average length of time a viewer looks at an image
they encounter in passing is three seconds.
Ouch.

Given that depressing factoid, the artist is faced with a challenge: to keep the viewer's eye on the page long enough to tell your story. The trick is to keep things moving: as soon as the eyes settle into place with nothing pulling at them, boredom sets in and the battle is lost.

One solution lies in *continuation of form*—placing forms and spaces in a way that suggests an unbroken line chaining together the key parts of an image, carving a path of least resistance between them for the observer to follow. In particular, anything that catches the eyes as they wander off the edges and redirects them back to the center of the image is solid gold.

Making the visual path a closed circuit can encourage onlookers to do multiple laps through a piece, hitting each stop on the loop a number of times. Add in sub-loops and other detours, and the time it takes to complete each lap goes up accordingly, racking up precious seconds of viewing time for your opus. Giant arrows are an obvious way of directing attention, but the eye will pick up on surprisingly subtle cues—sometimes subliminal suggestion is the most powerful kind. So long as the path remains clear and logical, the audience will follow it.

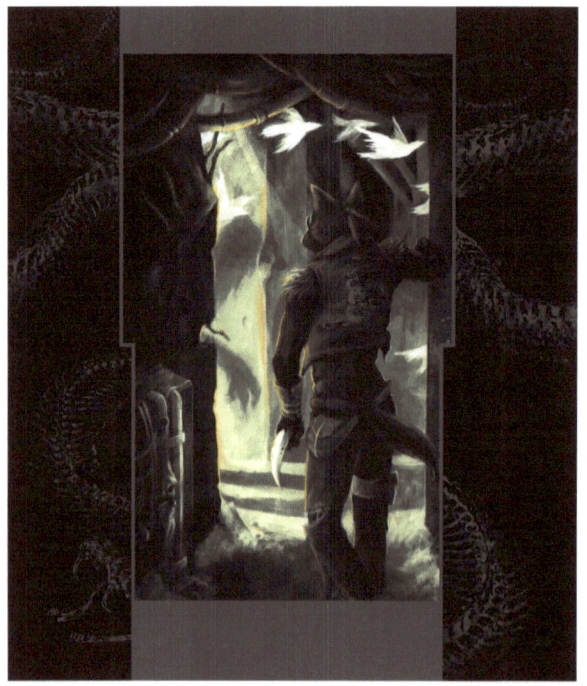 =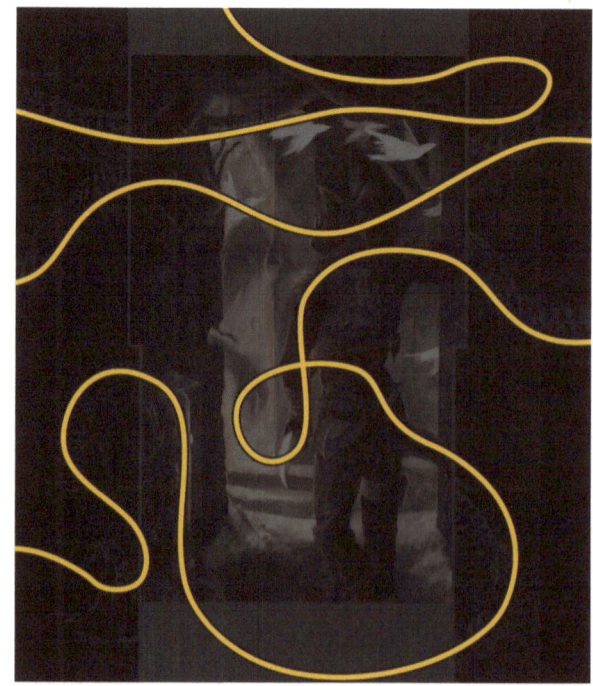

Spaghetti!

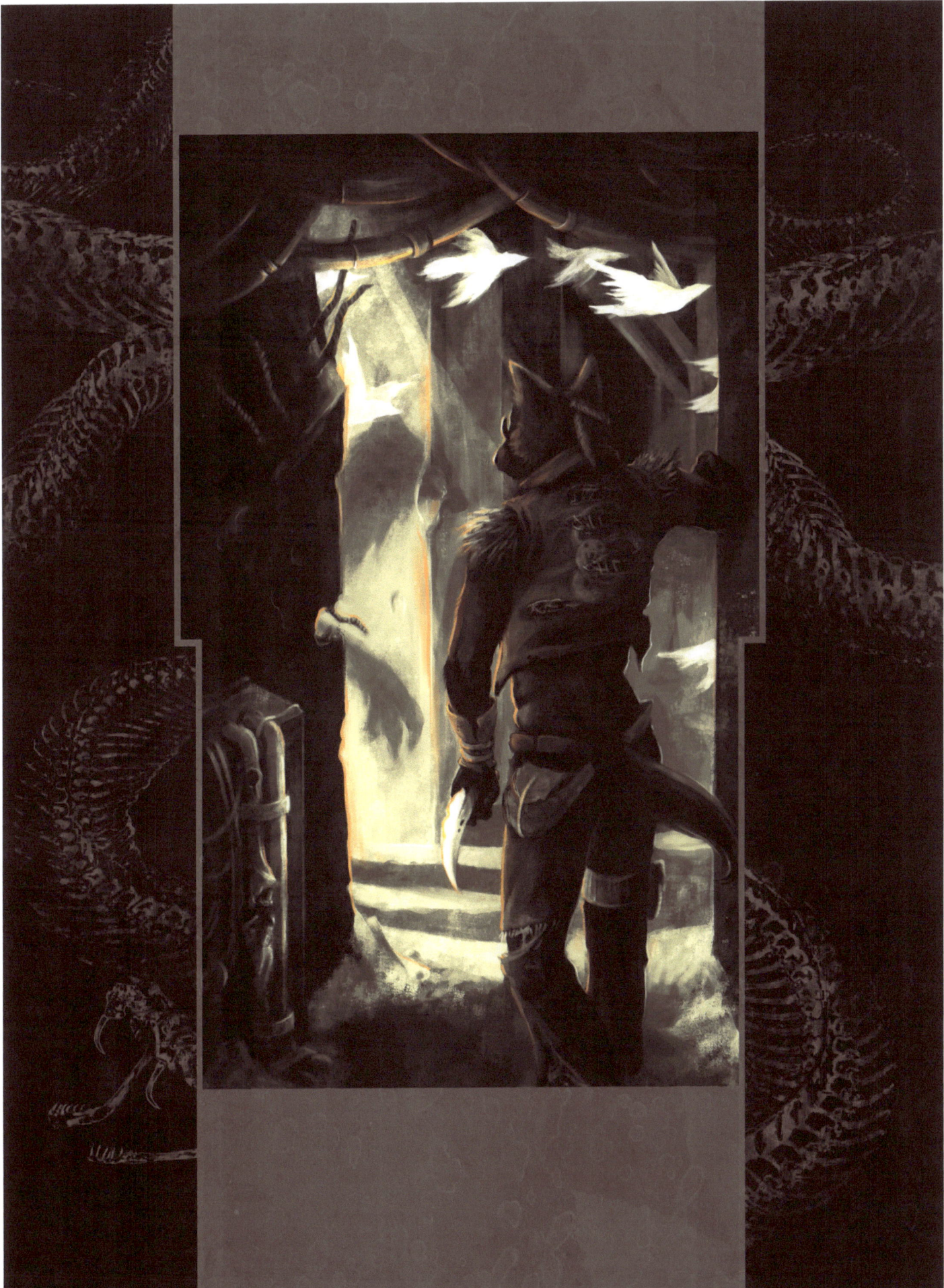

Every picture tells a story, but not every image needs to be an epic. If you *do* want to pack a lot of narrative in, though, make sure each detail is pitching in.

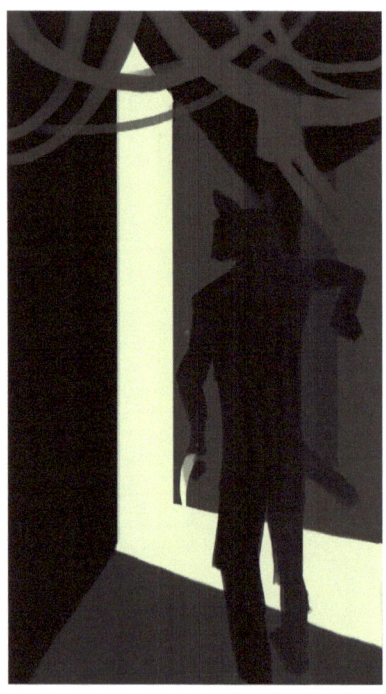

This illustration was for the cover of a post-apocalyptic sci-fi novel, so I wanted to really push that visually.

The point was to construct a scene that would get across the atmosphere and context more than it was to showcase a specific character, so I made sure to build the image as a whole from the onset. The background is just as important as the figure here, and they needed to really marry.

Not making backgrounds an afterthought is always a good idea, but in this case, it was especially important.

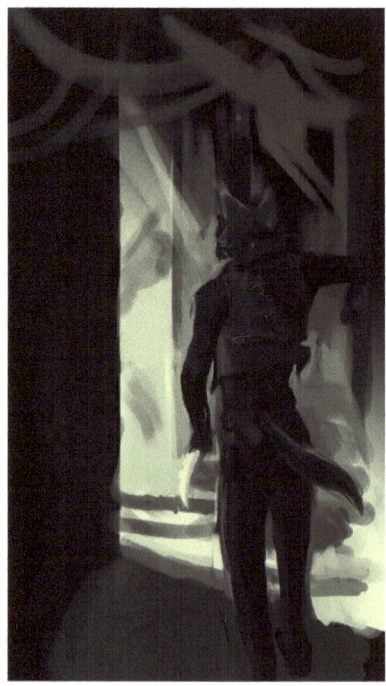

The mood I wanted to get across was tension and suspense, but in the middle of the eerie quiet and serenity that you find in ruins.

I used the idea of not knowing what lies around the corner in a literal way here, with a sinister shadow that suggests the answer is likely "nothing friendly."

The figure's pose is saying ready for action, but relaxed—as if to suggest that they're so used to these encounters that they don't brace up when confronted with them any more.

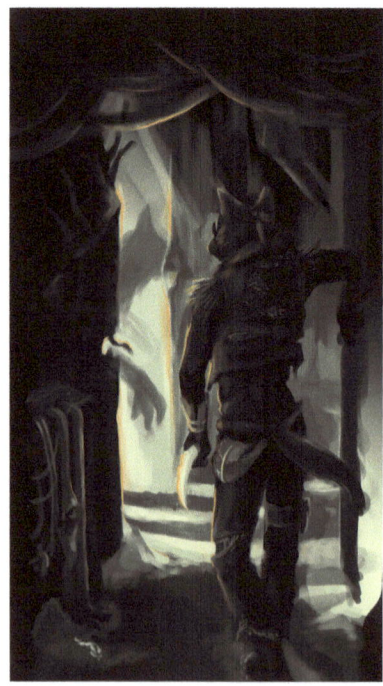

Cables, pipes, and tubes all make for interesting curves, while also being associated with civilization. Seeing those things hang limp or broken speaks to the fallen state of this society.

Bits of broken, eroded concrete suggest that things have been broken for long while now, and the piles of dust indicate that the area doesn't get much traffic.

Whatever's around that corner, this guy is on his own.

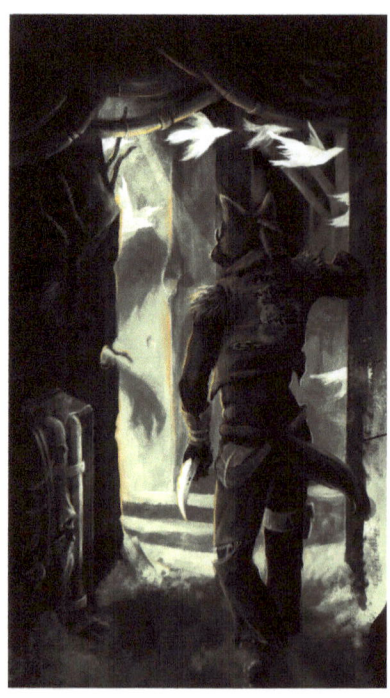

Diffuse lighting that catches the dust in the air softens the scene some, while the white birds give it some fast action.

It's a pretty still scene, and you get the impression that the shadow is drawing closer slowly (as in any good thriller flick), so I figured the burst of noise and action from the birds flapping past would make for a startling but beautiful contrast.

Even though the figures still haven't made contact, and the protagonist is safely hidden for now around the corner, I wanted to emphasize that this creature was just moments away.

Having the shadow almost touch the main figure helps to give them that sense of tension, and having the snout's shadow bend around the wall is a visual anticipation of when the thing that's casting it also turns the corner.

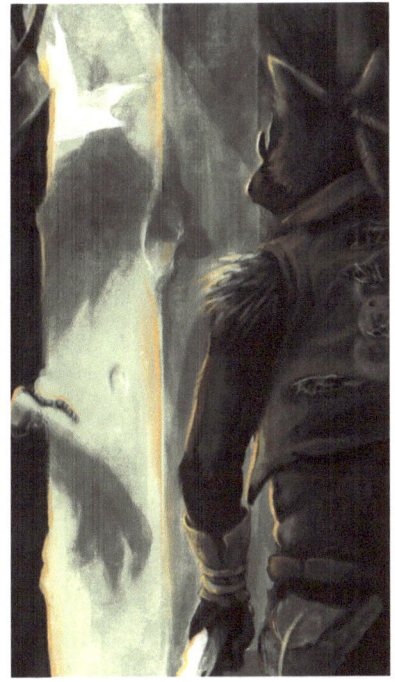

For the watermark on the frame holding the image, I wanted to use something iconic.

I thought that a venomous snake would add a nice sense of danger, and be appropriate to the sandy, desert setting, but decided it was a little *too* threatening.

Instead, I chose to go with the remains of said serpent. It still references the danger, but adds a sense of the indiscriminate mortality that goes along with the post-apocalyptic genre.

You don't have the immediate fear that the page is going to bite you, but you get to thinking, *"Wow, if even a pit viper can't survive here, how is the average Joe supposed to hack it?"*

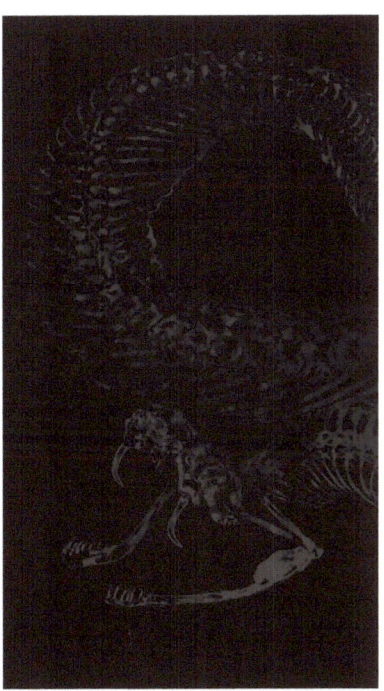

Adding an eroded, oxidized metal texture to the frame helped age it, and reinforces the idea of a city that's been left unattended and exposed to the elements for several years.

There's a lot going on in this image, but everything is at least hopefully sending the same message.

Just like a large chorus of voices works as long as everybody's saying the same thing at the same time, you can get away with making an image pretty busy so long as you choose your details thoughtfully.

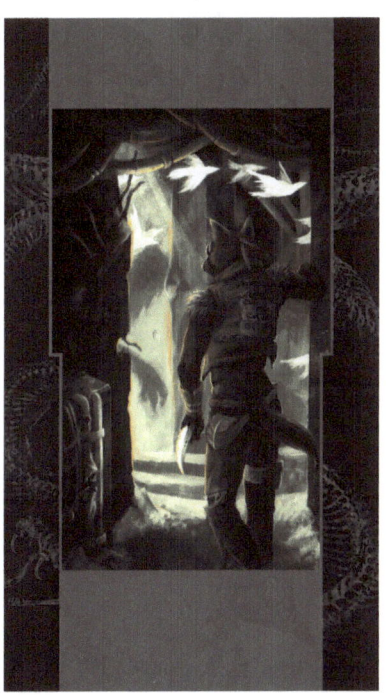

Knives? Doves in slow motion? What is this, a John Woo movie?

39

the hero
research

If it's all been done before, the trick is to find out who did it best.
Why ~~steal~~ *draw influence* from anything less?

For this piece, a prospective cover for some historical fiction, I wanted the image to evoke the period in which the piece was set. Stained glass windows had their beginnings in crusade-era medieval churches, so I felt it was an appropriate style for the illustration. Though the works of the time were often basic, the crusade-themed designs that ornamented subsequent cathedrals feature breathtaking detail and rich colors.

Aspiring to that, I decided to do some homework before diving into the sketch. Enabled by the magic of Google™, I took a quick world tour looking at stained glass windows, examining how the light filtered through them, what happens to the colors, etc. I also looked into artists famous for their work in stained glass, ranging from Albrecht Dürer to William Morris.

In addition to being fascinating and beautiful and inspiring, that helped me execute the image in a way that was more authentic to the medium than I could have managed on my own. The imagination is a powerful image-building tool, but sometimes hard facts and the experience of others can help you push your own abilities farther. Tracing reference images will get you nowhere, but learning from the masters is always a great exercise in developing your own art.

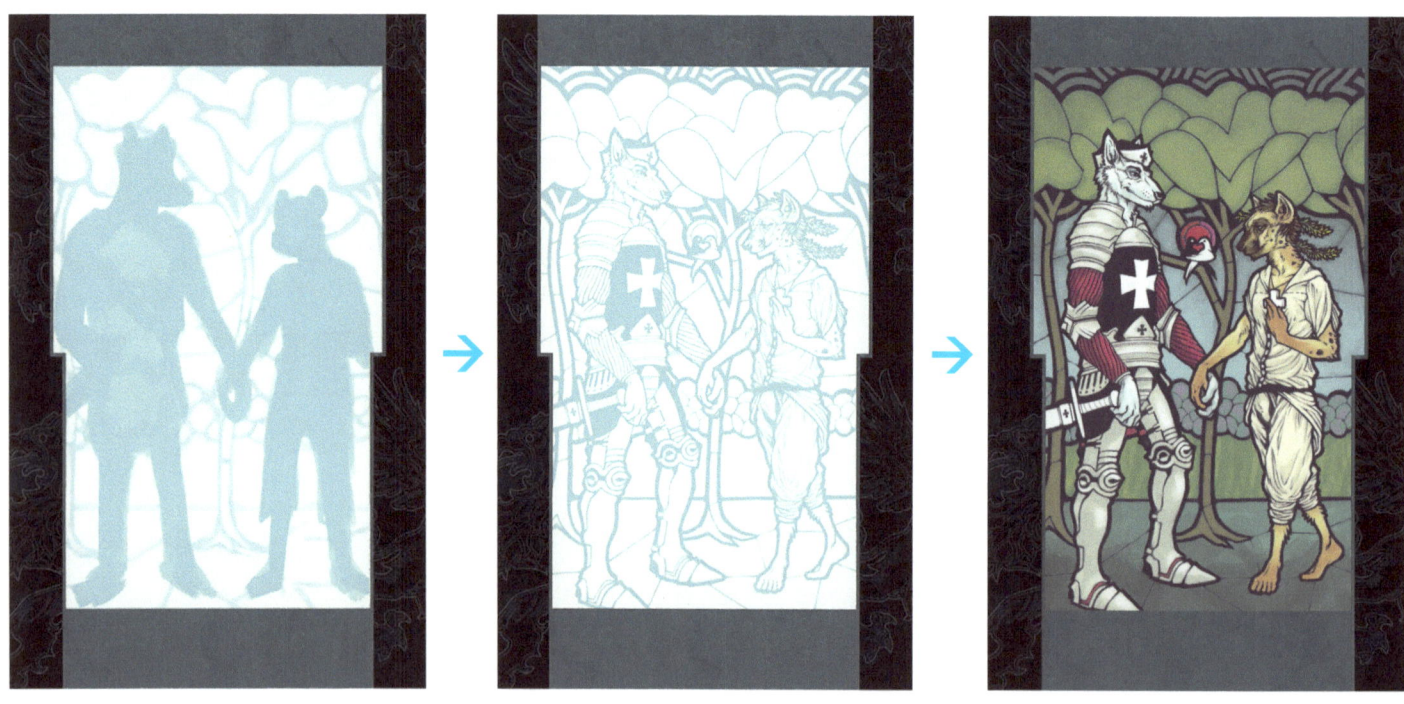

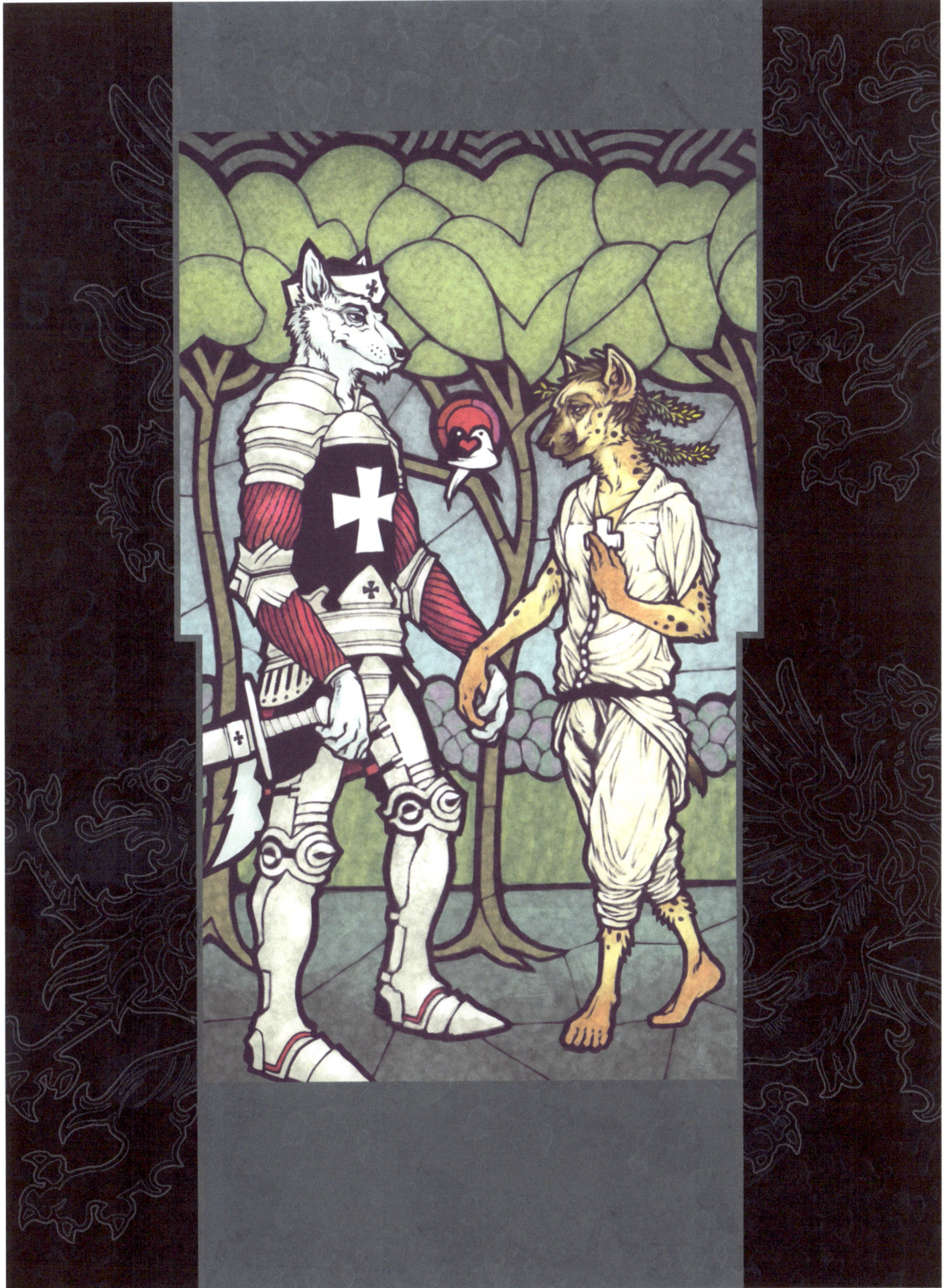

Let's get back to the technical for a bit. Sometimes you want to fill an area with color or pattern, need it to stay inside the lines, and want to be able to move it around later. Well, rest easy. Layer masks have your back.

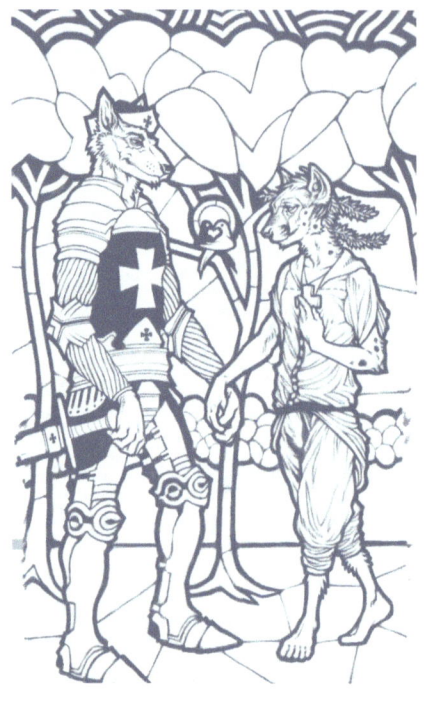

If we want to learn a new way to stay inside the lines when coloring an image, we'll need to start with some lines.

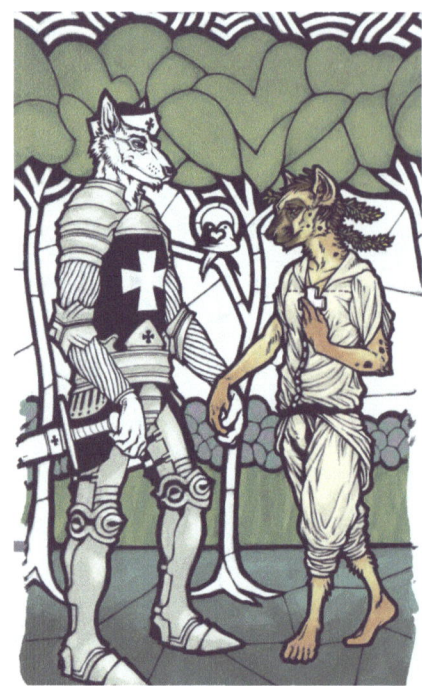

I'm making new color layers under my lines layer as I add in portions of color. The lines are fairly broad, so keeping the color areas inside the boundaries isn't too difficult.

So what do you do when you *are* dealing with fine boundaries? Well, that's an issue I ran into when working on the frame.

I start with this—a big flat pattern, made from a gryphon print with a texture layer over it. You can't see it here, but it continues off the canvas on both sides.

I know that I like the gryphons, but I don't know exactly where I want to place them yet, relative to the image.

I need to create a window in this layer to allow my painting underneath to show through, so I start by creating a selection in the right shape.

At this point, I could just hit delete to clear the pixels inside that selection and be done with it, but then what happens if I don't like where the gryphons are lying on the page?

By clearing pixels, I would be permanently removing all of that information, which ties the position of the window to the pattern.

It's in times like these that layer masks offer a better way!

42

With that selection still active, I head over to my layers palette and click on the Add layer mask button (boxed in orange here).

All of a sudden, everything BUT the window I wanted to cut out disappears. Ugh!

It's cool. What I've done is masked off everything outside of my selection. Next to the layer thumbnail, a black and white image appears that represents my mask—black areas mean that part of the layer is hidden, white areas mean those parts show up.

So how do we flip the frame around to the way we want it? Just click on that black and white thumbnail on your layer, then hit CTRL+I to invert the colors, changing black to white and white to black, and presto!

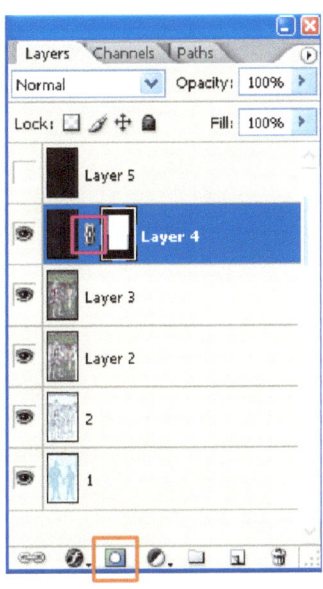

It's a little confusing at first, but the fact that layer masks can be edited on the fly using painting tools is *awesome*.

So, back to my little gryphon problem. When I try moving the frame layer around, I run into the same issue as before—the window is locked to the pattern, so moving one means moving the other.

Back up to the layers palette again, and check out the little chain icon between the layer thumbnail and the mask thumbnail (boxed in pink in the image to the left).

Click on that and it will disappear. Now let's try moving the gryphons again...

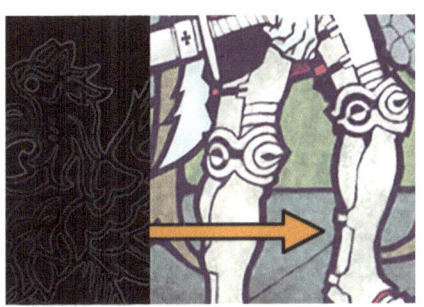

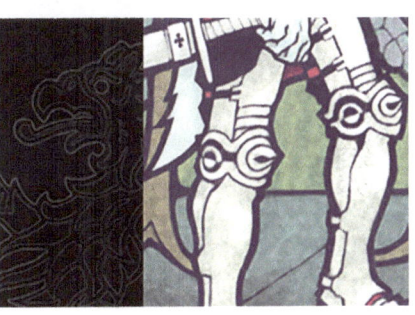

Perfect! Now I can move the gryphon print around as much as I want while keeping the masked-off portion still.

It's a little trippy, but extremely useful in cases like these.

Gryphons settled into place, I'm ready to do some final color and texture adjustments, use the dodge tool to add in some hot spots where the sunlight shining through my imaginary stained glass illustration would be extra bright, and it's all done!

SHIFT-clicking a mask will toggle it in a move I like to call "mask on, mask off." It's way Zen.

lucky red
lighting

And he said, "Let there be light!"
And I was all, "Oh, sure, easy for *you* to say!"
...Jerk.

Ahem... Getting back on track: strong lighting can serve to set a mood, tie together a disparate color scheme by introducing a common tone across the board, and boost contrast. The soft yellow-green of dappled sunlight filtering through tree leaves can make a picture calm and soothing, while the stark, pale blue of fluorescent institutional lighting can make a scene feel cold and sterile. For this image, I wanted a sultry, spicy bedroom scene, so I went with cheap bordello red.

In general, tinted light will lend its color to any surface that catches it; more visibly on lighter colored surfaces than dark ones, and in proportion to that surface's reflectivity. Smooth, moist, or metallic objects are more highly reflective than others, so they are more heavily influenced by the brightness and color of the light they catch. Rougher objects with a dull, matte finish will pick up less of the light and retain more of their original color. A surface's reflectivity also determines how much light it bounces back onto neighboring objects. That bounced light can hit things that aren't directly exposed to the original source at all—light has a sneaky way of creeping into every corner of a scene.

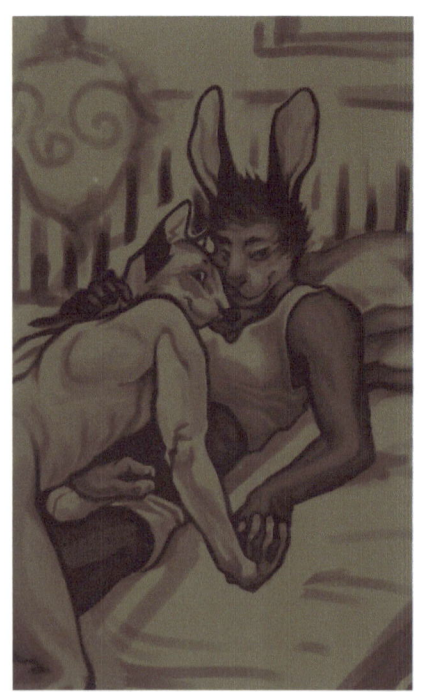 + 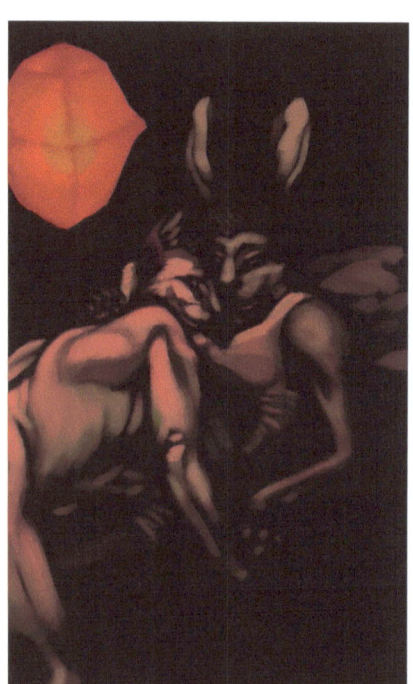 →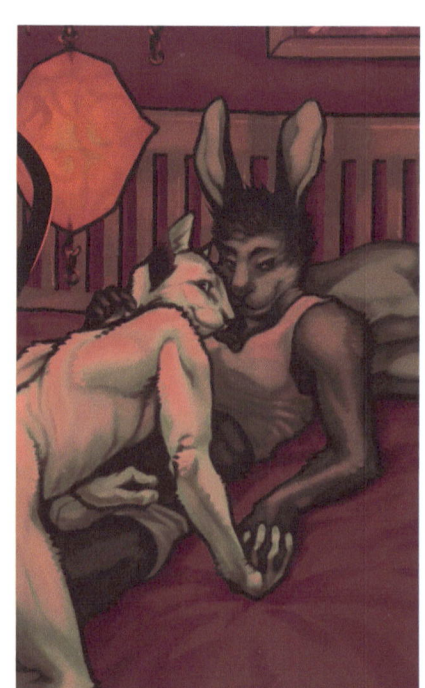

44

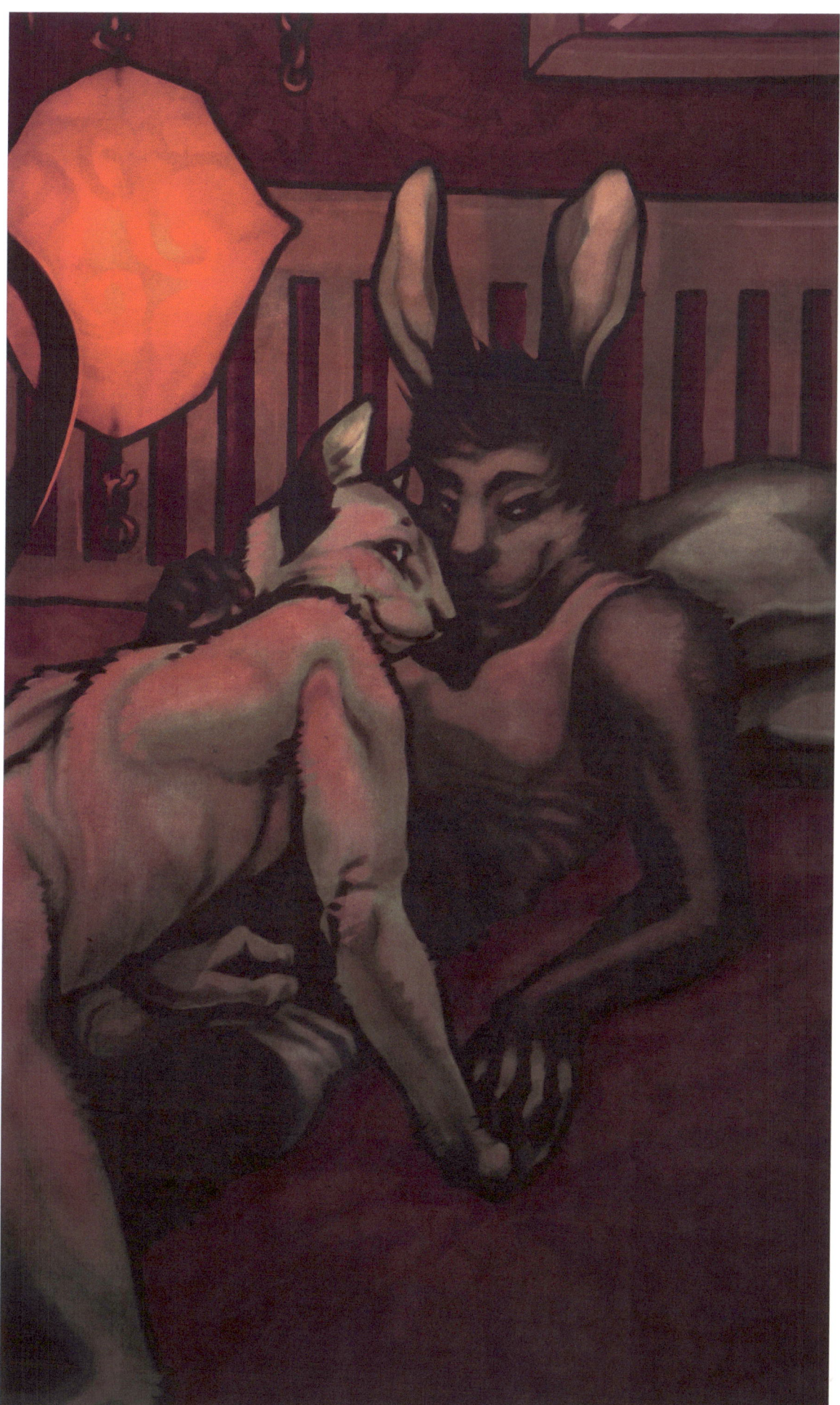

Even a dull image can be brought to life with vivid lighting. Knowing how you want to light a scene from the get-go is great, but it's never too late to help an illustration shine.

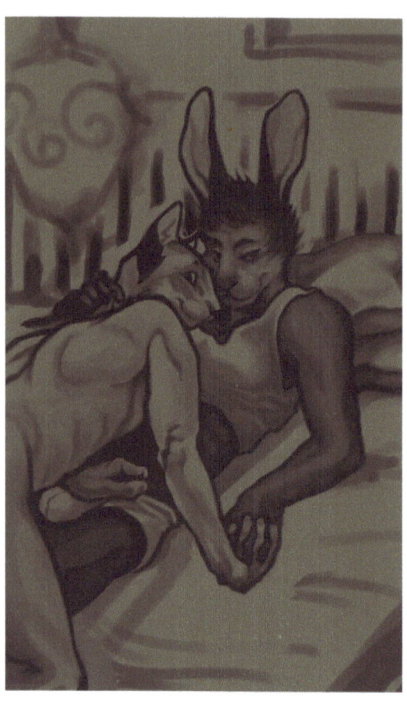

Light affects everything about a scene, from the way the forms and values work together to create the illusion of dimension to the angle that shadows are cast.

Keeping a solid mental picture of where and what your light sources are when painting from the sketch phase will help you illuminate your images more convincingly.

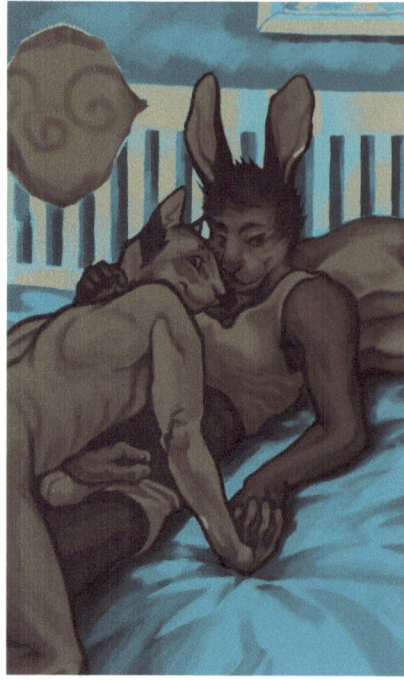

Before I hit on ho-bag red as the thematic color for this piece, I started painting in one of my familiar greyish blues. When that wasn't giving off the mood I wanted, I decided to change things up.

So what happens to the time I spent painting the sheets (and why do people laugh when I ask that question)?

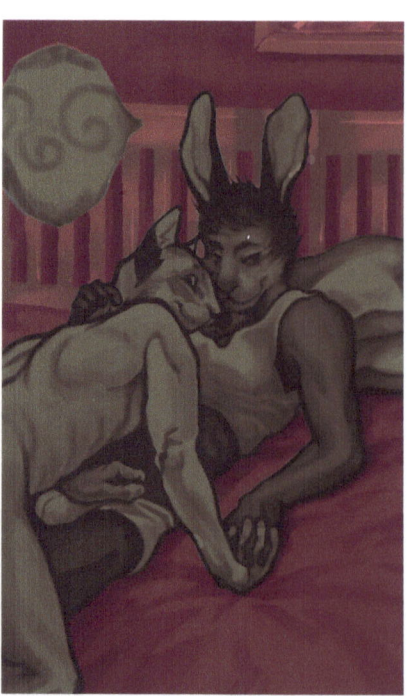

This happens! The Gradient Map feature (Image > Adjustments > Gradient Map) can be a wonderful way of trying out new color schemes on existing paintings.

It works by matching up ("*mapping*") the darks and lights in your image (regardless of their current color) to the colors along a gradient you determine. By default, the darkest value in your existing image will be replaced with the color at the left end of the gradient you make, the lightest with the color at the far right, and everything in between accordingly.

Click on the gradient to edit it, and watch the results change in real time as you go (as long as the Preview box is checked).

Gradient Map has the major advantage over some of other color-shifting features in that you can very specifically change multiple colors in your image at the same time with no regard to their original hue.

Conversely, because it relies on value (how light or dark a color is), areas of the same value but different hue which looked totally different before will all get mapped as the same color.

Which tool you use depends on the image in question—try playing with the Gradient Map until you get a feel for its strengths and limitations.

46

Now that I know I'm going red, I'm ready to drop in the light source and paint in some of the cast light.

I used a new layer on top of my base painting so I could make any adjustments to the lighting while leaving the figures underneath intact if I changed my mind later.

The image to the right shows my light layer on top of a black layer I added here so it's easier to see what's going on. While painting, I worked directly over the image so I could see what I was doing.

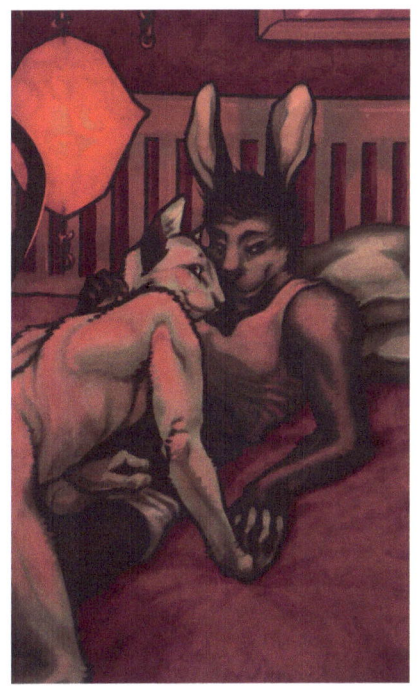

Here's what I was seeing.

I added some white to the lighting on the cat to distinguish him from the bunny a bit more, who I kept the same dark olive brown.

I've also added a pattern layer to the sheets and wallpaper to give it a bit more texture, and added some chunky arabesques to the silk lantern.

The lighting seemed a bit too uniform at this point, and the lower-right corner was feeling pretty dead, so I decided to throw a simple lighting effect on the stack.

Making a new layer, I used the gradient tool centered around the lamp to make a quick radial gradient from white to a cool blue tone.

I then duplicated this layer, and set the bottom copy's blending mode to Multiply and the top one to Color. The former will darken the image more and more the further out from the light it gets (because white is invisible in a Multiply layer), while the latter saps more and more of the red out.

That creates the illusion that the red light, very intense near its source, quickly dissipates the further out it goes.

That's in keeping with what you'd expect from a little silk lantern, so it looks more convincing, and also helps to set a more intimate mood for the scene.

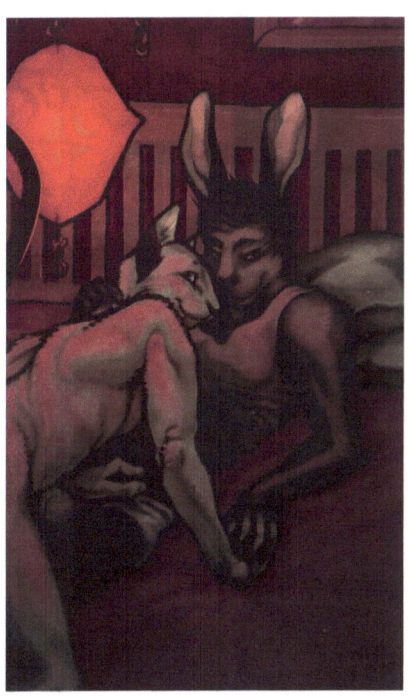

The ugliest guy in any dark bar knows that the right lighting can make all the difference.

slim charlie
finishing

So, here we are.

In trying to decide how to end this collection, I thought it might be interesting to talk about how I finish the images I work on. Once the paint's been laid, the textures tweaked, I go through a series of final adjustments that are as much a ceremony for me as they are a way to polish the image for presentation. I could easily spend weeks poking and prodding away at an illustration, massaging it in this way or that on a level so fine that nobody but me would ever notice, so learning to call a piece *done* is important.

While I'll share the specific filters I run my images through on their way out the gate here, I encourage everyone—digital artists and real media folk, writers, poets, all of you—who has trouble letting go sometimes to develop a similar ritual for themselves. It sounds corny, I know, but it's easy to get attached to a piece, and breaking up is hard to do.

Learning to push on to new territory will not only up your productivity (in my experience, the first 90% of an image constitutes about 50% of the total time. Getting from 99.5 to 99.9% can take forever, and I don't think I've ever seen 100% before.), but it will keep you working on fresh themes, trying new techniques, exploring new styles. You'll stay more sane for it, and I'll wager your art will grow a lot faster in the process. Happy trails, folks!

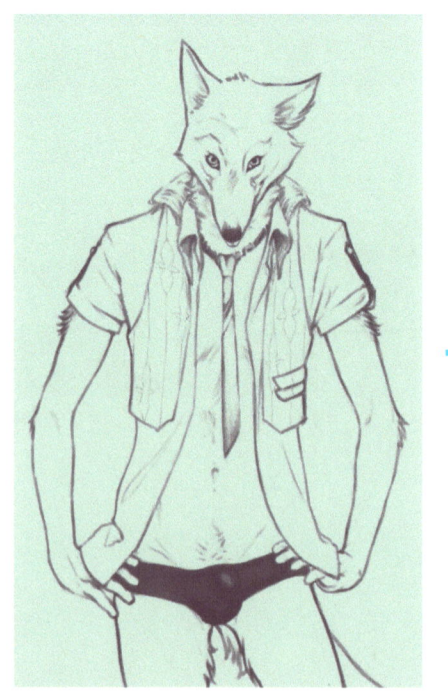 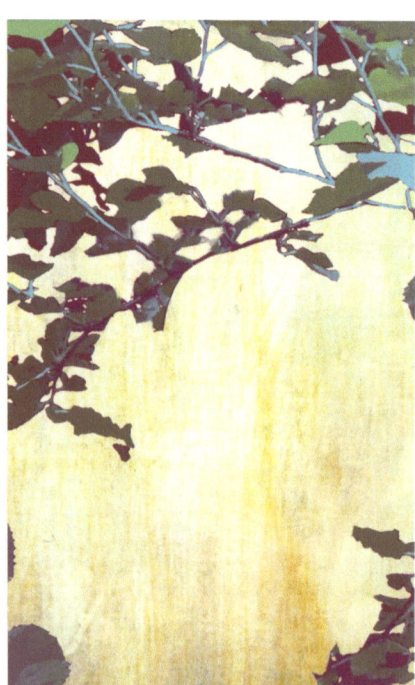 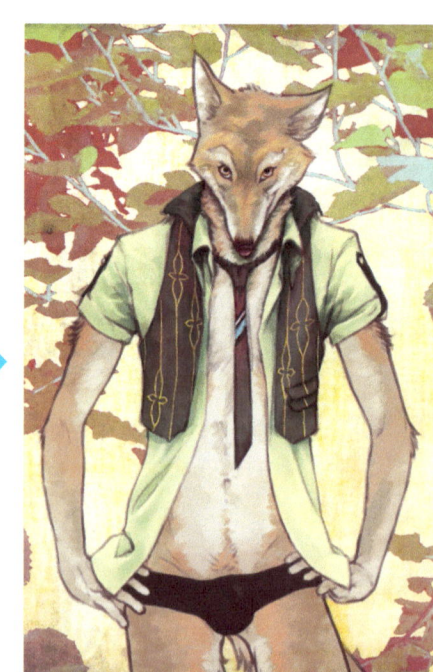

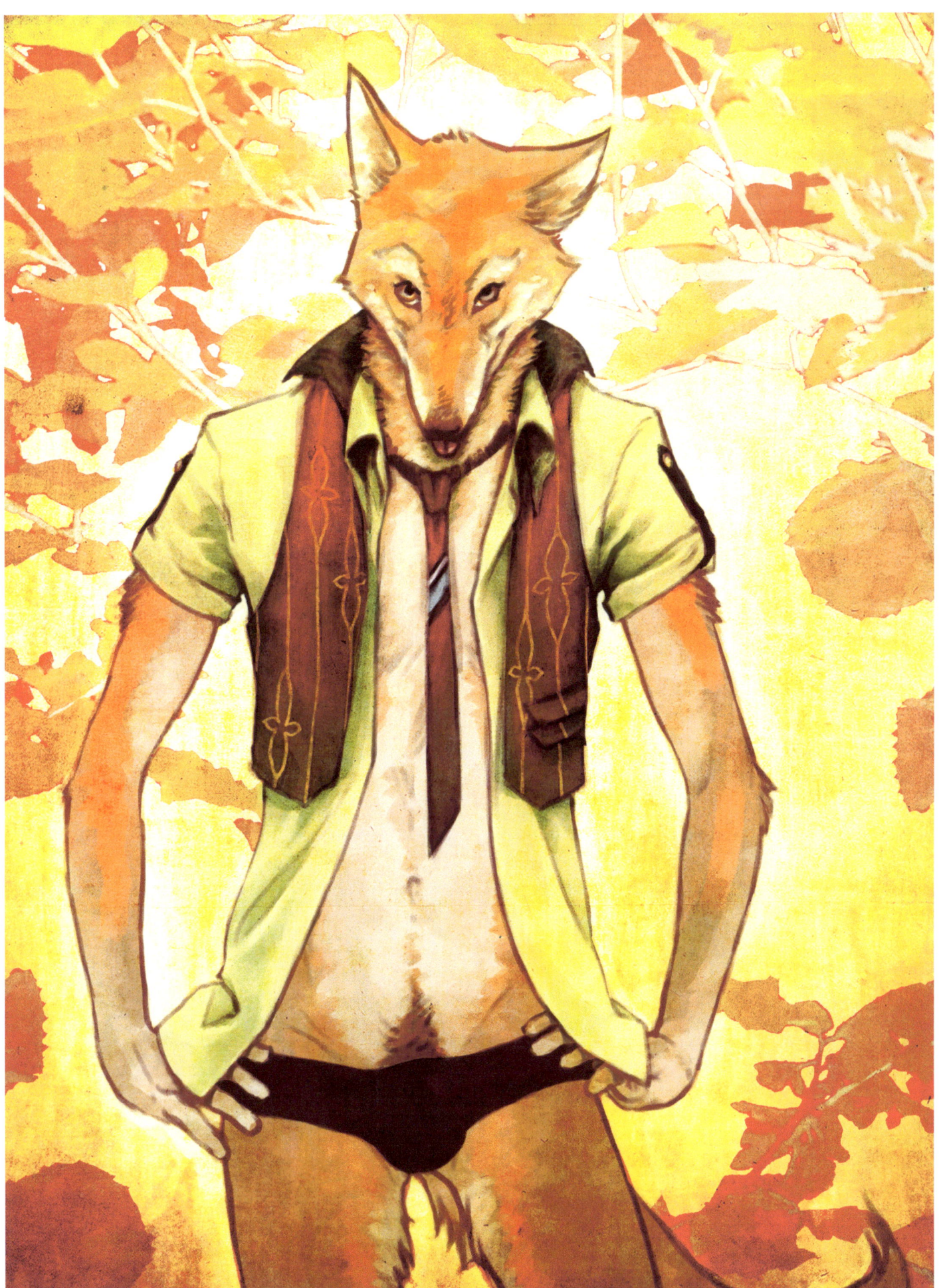

It's finally done. You're through painting your image, and you're all set to publish it. Well, sit tight just a bit longer. Here's how I put that finishing polish on my work.

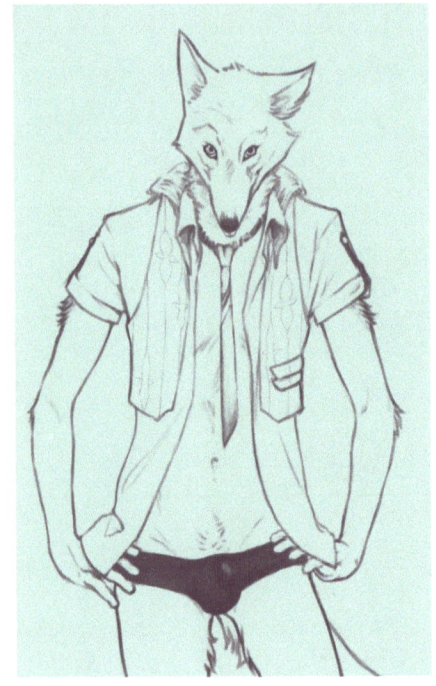

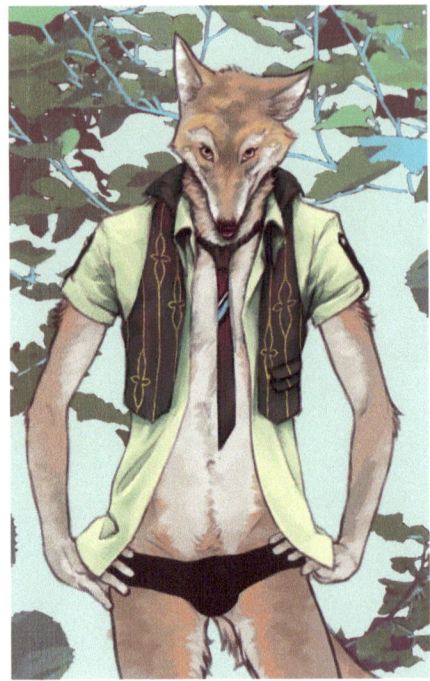

I suppose you have to start an image in order to finish it, but we'll cheat this time and just cut to the chase.

Here's the finished linework.

I painted in a few branches and leaves behind him in various woodsy shades of green, red, and brown, and used similar tones in his outfit.

Even though most of the hues here fall into a harmonious color family in theory, problems with contrast are making things a little rough on the eyes.

No worries, though—all the info is there. Now all we have to do is massage it some until everything clicks into place.

CTRL+B or Image > Adjustments > Color Balance will bring you to this dialogue.

Select among shadows, midtones, and highlights in the tone balance section, then play with the sliders to adjust the colors in your image.

The further toward either extreme you push the slider, the more you'll bring out that color within your image.

I usually wind up making extremely fine adjustments on the order of ±2 or 3 when I'm doing this at the end of a piece, but I'll often use it in heftier doses earlier on.

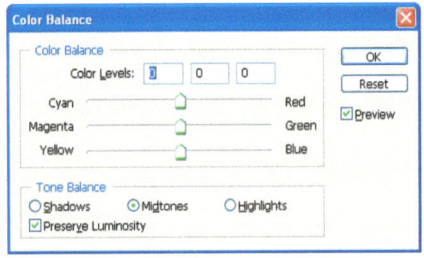

Now that our colors are properly balanced, it's time to balance our values with the help of the Levels feature (CTRL+L or Image > Adjustments > Levels).

The mountain range pictured here is a histogram showing the relative concentrations of all the values in your image, but you don't really need to know that.

See the three little carrots below the histogram? Sliding the outer two inwards will darken your darks and lighten your lights respectively. Moving the middle one will shift around your mid-tones.

If you feel like your shadows are a little flat, or your highlights a little dull, here's where to go.

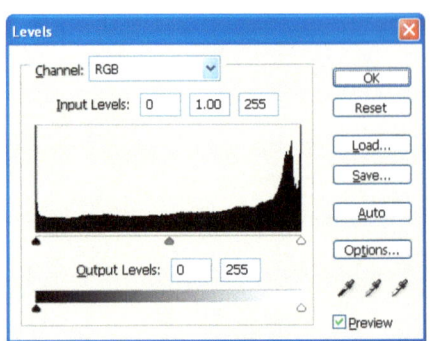

50

That takes care of our hues and values—all that's left is to balance the saturation!

CTRL+U or Image > Adjustments > Hue/Saturation will get you this dialogue box, but I find that the hue slider here is a little limited in usefulness because it shifts every color in your image at once, rather than allowing for the selective changes you can make with Color Balance.

Likewise, the lightness slider pales in comparison to the Levels feature.

The Saturation slider is the big winner here. If all of your colors are seeming washed out, crank it up! Or, if they're a little too atomic, you can ratchet them back down.

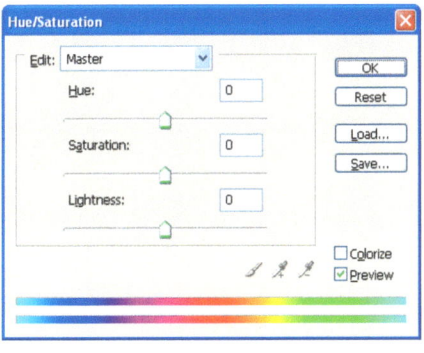

So let's see these things in action.

I like all the different colors that were happening here on a one-by-one basis, but there are so many that it's getting pretty busy.

Color Balance to the rescue!

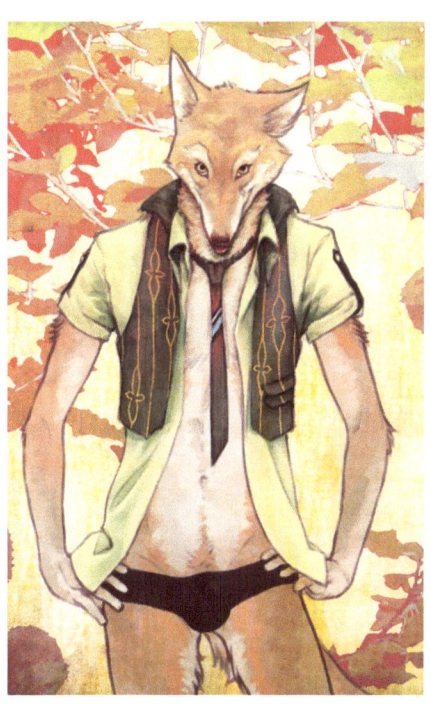

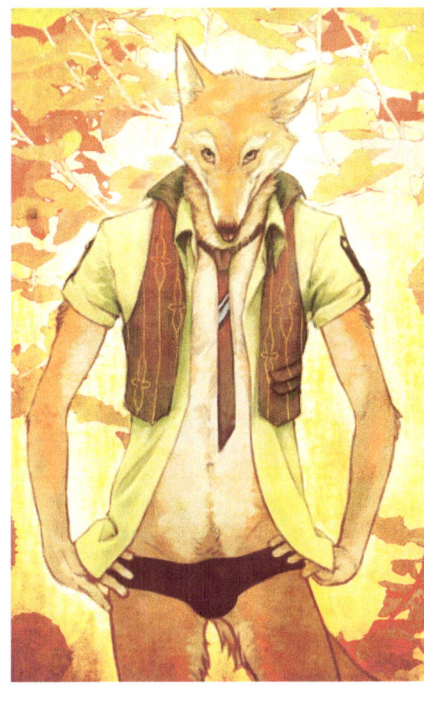

In Color Balance, I pushed all the different hues toward a golden russet target. That unified them some, making the image calmer visually.

The result seems a bit washed out, though. Nothing that Levels and Hue/Saturation can't fix, though.

Using Levels, I got those shadows back to a nice, clear, deep tone that helps lift the figure off the background.

Then I cranked up the saturation to bursting. All of those golds and oranges refuse to be muted. This kid is full-on electric!

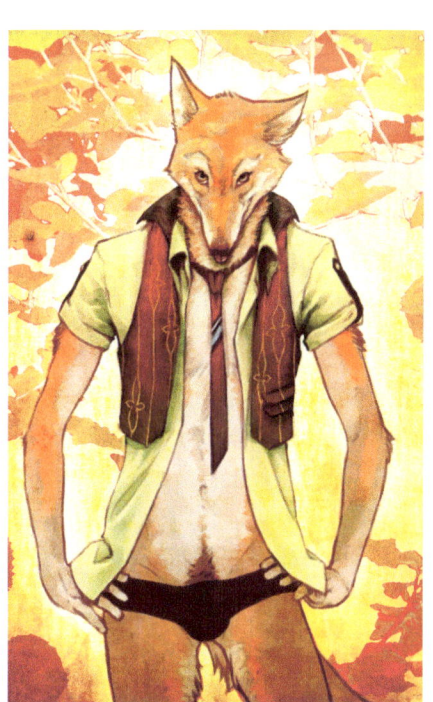

Some might call my neurotic color balancing a little silly. I call it love.

51

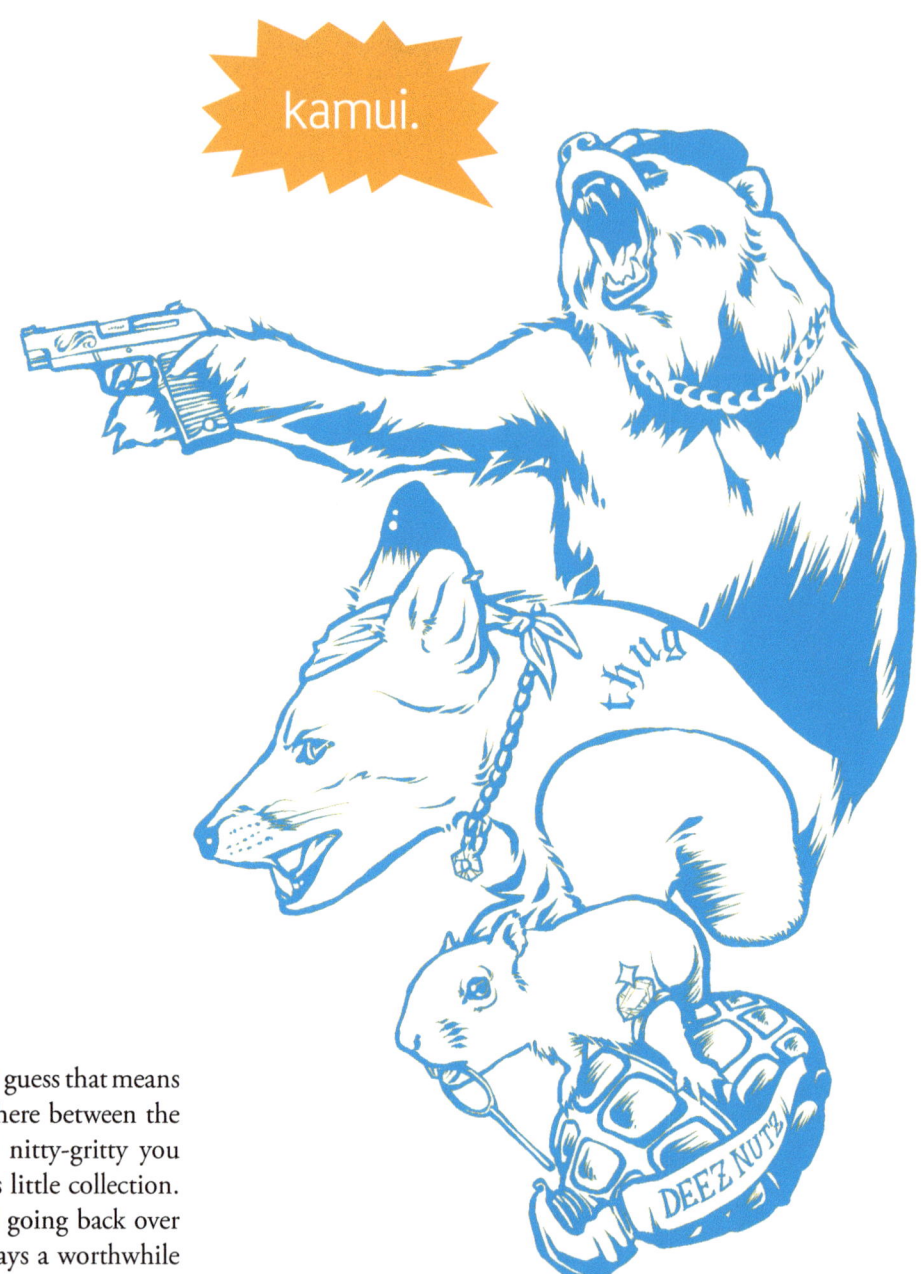

Afterword

Well, I'm fresh out of slides here—I guess that means the fun's over. I hope that somewhere between the finished pieces and the technical nitty-gritty you found something enjoyable in this little collection. It was a blast to put together, and going back over the basic rules and theories is always a worthwhile thing, regardless of your level of experience.

My egotistical hope is that, at least for a short while before making its migration to the bookshelf, this book gets to sit open beside you as you make some art of your own. Even if it never comes around to me, I'll be happy to think that there's been a reply from the void.

Thanks, and happy arting!

www.ingramcontent.com/pod-product-compliance
Lightning Source LLC
Chambersburg PA
CBHW051218220526
45473CB00003B/1085